Celebrating the Seder

Celebrating the Seder

A resource for a Christian
interpretation of the Passover meal

Nick Fawcett

First published in 2004 by
KEVIN MAYHEW LTD
Buxhall, Stowmarket, Suffolk IP14 3BW
E-mail: info@kevinmayhewltd.com

Scripture quotations are the author's own paraphrase.

9 8 7 6 5 4 3 2 1 0

ISBN 1 84417 330 5
Catalogue Number 1500746

Cover image: Detail from Chasuble with 'Chalice and Grapes' design
available from Kevin Mayhew Church Requisites
Cover design by Angela Selfe
Edited by Katherine Laidler
Typesetting by Richard Weaver

Printed and bound in Great Britain

Contents

Introduction

Why celebrate a seder meal? Isn't the Jewish Passover from which it originates part of a different faith tradition, rooted in Old Testament history, and distant history at that? The answer, of course, is yes, and that fact counsels caution and respect when organising any Passover-related activity. For Jews across the world this is a sacred occasion, recalling an event integral not just to their past but to their present – an event that has shaped their understanding of God and of themselves as a people. We need to recognise that and treat any seder celebration, albeit one adapted to a Christian context, with the dignity it deserves. Equally, we must remember that we are not celebrating the Passover as such, for we approach the meal from a Christian perspective, which inevitably influences our understanding of what it means.

Yet the Old Testament is part of Christian as well as Jewish tradition – though all too often a sadly neglected one. A seder ceremony reminds us of our joint roots, a common inheritance in which, of course, Jesus himself shared. In its own right, the story of God delivering his people from Egypt is one that deserves to be told, for it has so much to teach us concerning God's gracious redemptive purpose, and indeed regarding the evil and inhumanity that scars our world today as much as in years gone by. To learn about what God has done in the arena of human history can surely only deepen and enrich our faith, and if it leads also to greater respect for the Jewish tradition, then that is an added bonus. For Christians, though, no reason should be needed for linking a seder meal to Christian worship, for the precedent was set by Jesus himself in the last supper he shared with his disciples. When he broke bread and shared wine, he did so at Passover, clearly intending us to interpret his words and actions in terms of that festival. As the new Paschal lamb, he tells us, he brings freedom through the shedding of his blood, deliverance from all that holds us captive, a new and living relationship with God.

The aim of this book is to provide a resource through which we, as Christians, can learn from the Passover tradition, fully respecting what it means within Judaism but building upon it in terms of our own tradition. I begin with a seder that follows the customary pattern of Passover, making no conscious attempt to interpret this in terms of Christian convictions. Suitably adapted, this could serve as a demonstration meal, if desired. The second seder incorporates all the main features of a traditional Passover meal, but develops certain aspects in the light of Christ, concluding with a celebration of the Eucharist. The remaining seders, which also culminate in the Eucharist, each pick up one of the four key teaching strands integral to the Passover, focusing upon this and using it to enlarge upon the meaning of the gospel and the relationship between the two. Finally, I provide two appendices, one offering a few simple recipes for a full seder meal and the other giving useful websites where traditional and Christian seders can be found.

My aim in writing this book has been to contribute in some small way to a fuller appreciation among Christians of both the Passover and the Lord's Supper. In doing so, I have attempted to respect fully the integrity of both, but if I have unwittingly misrepresented the content and symbolism of either, or in any way caused offence to the Jewish readers, I apologise unreservedly in advance. If I have succeeded, on the other hand, in helping to build bridges that might lead to dialogue and further reflection, then my purpose, at least in part, has been accomplished.

NICK FAWCETT

Meaning of Hebrew terms

afikoman Originally the last fragment of the Paschal lamb eaten at the close of the Passover meal, this today is represented by bread, broken from the central piece of unleavened bread and hidden until the end of the meal.

beitzah A roasted egg (often replaced today by a hard-boiled brown egg), used to symbolise both burnt offerings and new life.

chametz Bread made with leaven or yeast. The search for and eradication of this symbolises God's deliverance from all that corrupts and destroys within our lives.

charoset A concoction of honey, nuts, apples, cinnamon and wine. Its mud-like appearance recalls the time spent by the Israelites as slaves in Egypt, where they had to use mud mixed with straw as a form of cement and building material. The sweet taste of this mixture evokes the hope brought by faith in God, in contrast to the bitterness of oppression. To keep technical language to a minimum, I call this 'sweet paste' in the Christian seders.

chazeret A second bitter herb (often romaine lettuce), added to the maror. Together, these represent the bitterness of the Israelites' time of slavery in Egypt. In the Christian seders, I refer simply to 'bitter herbs'.

haggadah This refers to the written text of a seder.

hallel Meaning 'praise', this can refer to the section of the seder in which songs of worship are offered, or to the songs themselves.

hillel sandwich A symbolic element of the Passover meal, comprising two small pieces of unleavened bread, with bitter herbs (maror) and sweet paste (charoset) sandwiched between them.

k'arah An ornamental plate or tray on which the key elements of the seder are placed, these being (1) three 'loaves' of unleavened bread (matzot), (2) green vegetables (karpas), (3) a lamb bone (pesach), (4) bitter herbs (maror – and chazeret, if used), (5) a roasted egg (beitzah), and (6) charoset (the concoction of honey, nuts, apples, cinnamon and wine). In the Christian seders this is generally simply called a plate or ceremonial dish.

karpas   Vegetable or herb (parsley, lettuce, celery, raw cabbage, etc.), dipped in salty water. The salty water represents the tears of the Israelites during their time in Egypt, and reminds us that we too need to be set free from that which enslaves us. To keep things simple, I generally refer to this in the Christian seders as green vegetable.

kiddush   Sometimes rendered 'kadesh', this is a toast to freedom, celebrating the deliverance of Israel from captivity in Egypt.

maggid   This means 'retelling the story', and, as we shall see, this is traditionally done in a variety of ways.

maror   A bitter herb (traditionally horseradish, either grated or bought as horseradish sauce), used to symbolise the bitterness of slavery in Egypt.

matzah   Matzah (plural 'matzot') means unleavened bread; that is, bread made without yeast. It is central to the Passover tradition, recalling how the Israelites were commanded to be ready to leave Egypt at a moment's notice. Three matzot are used in the Passover Seder, two representing those placed in the Jerusalem Temple during the festival, and a further one being broken during the seder, part of it hidden as the afikoman and the other part placed on the ceremonial plate between the other two matzot. In the Christian seders I sometimes retain this term but sometimes simply use 'unleavened bread'.

pesach   Meaning 'Passover', this can refer to the Passover meal or festival in its entirety, or specifically, and more usually, to the Passover lamb. This lamb is typically represented in a seder meal by a lamb's roasted shank bone.

seder   This simply means 'order' but is occasionally used to refer to the first night of the Passover festival.

Background to the Passover

The origins of the Passover festival are to be found in the book of Exodus, specifically chapter 13, but to understand its significance we need to look back into Genesis, starting with the celebrated story of Joseph and his brothers. It was the imprisonment of Joseph in Egypt following the flirtatious advances of Potiphar's wife that set the stage for the single most significant event in Israel's event; an event still deeply rooted in the psyche of observant Jews today. Most people will probably have at least some knowledge of the bare bones of the story: how Joseph interpreted Pharaoh's dream after it had baffled the Egyptian soothsayers and mystics; how he subsequently rose to become Pharaoh's foremost official; how, in the wake of a catastrophic famine in Canaan, Joseph's father Jacob and his remaining sons set out for Egypt to buy food; how, finally reunited and reconciled with Joseph, they settled down in the land, multiplying and prospering to the point that, when a new Pharaoh replaced the old (the story now being taken up in the book of Exodus), he came to see them as foes rather than friends, an enemy within. So began an episode of ever-increasing oppression – a time tragically echoed so many times since in Jewish history – the Israelites being forced to work as slaves, labouring in the construction of Egypt's mighty buildings. Worse was to follow when Pharaoh gave the brutal order that all first-born sons of the Israelites should be killed. It was a time of abject despair and untold suffering in which faith, understandably, was tested to the limit, the Hebrews' cry for help seemingly ignored.

One child, however, had escaped the slaughter – the boy Moses. Set adrift in a wicker basket by his devoted mother, and subsequently found by Pharaoh's daughter among the bulrushes, he was raised in Pharaoh's household, reared there by his own mother, employed to nurse him. Clearly his mother left Moses in no doubt as to his true heritage, for in a fit of temper as a young man, he struck and killed an Egyptian whom he discovered beating a Hebrew slave, and was forced, as a result, to flee for his life into Midian. There came a moment while he was working as a shepherd for his father-in-law Jethro, that was to change not just his life but also that of his fellow-Israelites and, indeed, just about every Jew since, for, sensing God's presence in a burning bush, he received a call to return to Egypt and demand that Pharaoh release his people. It was not a call he relished, far from it; indeed, the prospect was so terrifying that he did all he could to wriggle off the hook, only finally agreeing to go if his brother Aaron could accompany him. The response of Pharaoh was all too predictable – a blanket refusal – and so began a series of ten plagues sent by God, designed to break the spirit of the Egyptians until Pharaoh had no option but to give way. The last of these plagues, in a tragic irony, was to be the death of the Egyptian first-born, Pharaoh's order to slaughter the first-born sons of the Israelites returning to haunt him.

In this last plague we come to the Passover itself. The Israelites were commanded to prepare unleavened bread in readiness to flee, and to slaughter a lamb, daubing its blood on the lintels of their homes. Thus would God's agent of death – whatever this actually was – *pass over* their houses. The carnage among the Egyptians that night was to be the straw that broke the camel's back: Pharaoh not only allowed but also ordered the Israelites to leave, heaping gold and jewellery upon them as a final incentive. A new chapter for the people had started – they were free! Yes, there were still testing moments to come, not least when Pharaoh changed his mind and sent an army to pursue them, but through it all Moses remained faithful, leading the people through the Red Sea and then on through long years in the wilderness, until at last they entered God's Promised Land, a land flowing with milk and honey.

This deliverance, then, is what Passover celebrates, doing so through a symbolic meal, the elements of which recall the bitterness of their captivity and joy of release. Otherwise known as the Feast of Unleavened Bread, it was originally almost certainly two festivals, the first being a spring ceremony aimed at shepherds and the latter a similar occasion for those involved in agriculture. In its emphasis on new beginnings, the festival in its current form still bears testimony to its early association with springtime, but these are now inextricably linked with those climactic events in Egypt through which God brought a fresh start to his people, and made possible the covenant between God and humankind effected shortly afterwards in the giving of the Ten Commandments.

Two key elements of a Passover meal are matzot (unleavened bread) and wine, as Jesus, being a Jew himself, would have been well aware. During his life he would have celebrated the Passover many times, so his sharing of supper with his disciples during the festival, and his interpretation of bread and wine within the seder, leave us in no doubt that he intended us to link the two, his death corresponding in some fundamental way to the sacrifice of the Passover lamb.

We need to be careful here not to misread the Jewish tradition in the light of Christian faith. The Jews *did* not and *do* not believe that the lambs killed on that first Passover night were being offered as a sacrifice to God, which, in itself, offered redemption – their understanding of the act was far more prosaic, demonstrating rather their obedience, trust and pride in being God's people. It was not the blood of the lamb that cleansed or purified people, but their devotion in following God's commandments.

When it comes to the meal Jesus shared on the Passover before his death, we are talking, of course, of the meal known today as the Lord's Supper. Just as blood needed to be shed prior to God inaugurating a unique covenant with his people, so, Jesus asserts, the shedding of his blood made possible a new covenant, God offering us not just liberation from physical captivity, wonderful though that is in itself, but freedom also from spiritual enslavement, from everything that undermines and destroys life, that keeps us from God, leading us astray and preventing us from being the people he wants us to be. In Christ God's promises made to his people of old are opened to all, not only a new chapter made possible but also a new creation, new life that extends beyond death into eternity.

Passover, then, is a living tradition. Still widely celebrated by Jews across the world in new and innovative ways as a reminder of God's faithfulness of old and his continuing purpose, it is also radically reinterpreted by Christians, re-enacted week by week as the Lord's Supper in recognition of what we believe God has done for us, and for all, through Christ. In both traditions, the symbolic meal and associated words are full of special meaning – making it indeed a seder worth celebrating.

Preparing for the meal

Types of meal

There are three ways in which a seder meal might be held.

- The first form is as a demonstration seder, in which case a traditional Passover pattern is followed as closely as possible. No attempt is made to introduce Christian elements – to do so would be disrespectful to Judaism, misrepresenting its most sacred of feasts, for however much *we* might believe the Passover finds its fulfilment in Christ, practising Jews, of course, think otherwise. The aim of a demonstration seder is to provide insight into what happens in the meal and why – a perfectly fitting objective given that the Old Testament is a shared Scripture for Christians and Jews alike. A demonstration seder, however, is not an act of worship and should not be seen as such; although participants might well sample the foodstuffs used in the meal, it is as part of a teaching exercise rather than an act of devotion. You could invite a local rabbi to conduct such a seder. Jewish synagogues also stage them on occasions.

- The second form is a symbolic seder. The traditional Passover pattern without the addition of any Christian elements could be followed, but more usually the latter are interwoven, the seder culminating in a celebration of the Lord's Supper. All the symbolic ingredients of the Passover meal are shared by participants – but this form of seder does not include a sit-down meal. It has the advantage of cutting down hugely on the amount of preparation needed, not to mention the work involved in serving and clearing up the meal afterwards. The downside, however, is that there is less time or opportunity to share sharing fellowship. Preparation may be less but it is nonetheless considerable, particularly if a large gathering is expected. In a small group, which perhaps best captures the original family feel of the occasion, participants can all recline around one table and take servings from a single dish of each of the foodstuffs used. A larger group will need several tables, each fully stocked and with leaders to break bread and serve as appropriate. If one table is used, each element of the meal needs to be duplicated so that participants can follow the leader's prompting and help themselves to the relevant footstuff during the meal. If there are several tables, each needs to be stocked with the necessary elements.

- The final form is a full seder meal. It is exactly the same as a symbolic seder except that a full meal is shared during the proceedings (recipes for this can be found in Appendix 1). Be warned that a seder of this kind will last for several hours. Ensure participants are aware of this. There are also cost implications, the food needing to be paid for. To cover this, and also to help those preparing the meal know approximately how many they will be catering for, you may decide to issue tickets for a full seder, these to be bought in advance of the meal.

The patterns given in this book can be used for either symbolic or full seder meals. For convenience, I refer to the leader in each case as 'he', but there is no reason why it should not be a 'she'.

Key food items

- Bitter herbs – horseradish, romaine lettuce, etc. (maror and chazeret)
- Green vegetables/herbs – parsley, lettuce, celery, etc. – (karpas)
- A mixture of chopped nuts, apples, cinnamon and wine (charoset)
- Unleavened bread (matzot) – three pieces for the leader to display and break, and three for each table (or participant)
- Bread (ordinary slices), to be broken in pieces and 'hidden' prior to the seder (leaven)
- An uncut loaf of bread (for use during the Lord's Supper)

(Note that, if more than one table is needed due to the number of participants, these items will need to be repeated on other tables. If this is the case, arrange the tables if possible in a U-shape, with the head table at the base of the U.)

Other items needed

For use by the leader

- Wine (or grape juice for those who prefer not to use alcohol)
- Four wine glasses or goblets (plus a fifth glass/goblet or chalice in Christian adaptations of the seder) – if you are following the traditional seder pattern closely, you will need an extra glass larger than the others, this representing the cup of Elijah. Traditionally, an empty place is set at the seder for Elijah

- A carafe (or carafes) for storing and pouring the wine
- A roasted or hardboiled egg (beitzah)
- An ornamental plate (k'arah)
- The roasted shank bone of a lamb (pesach)
- A bowl of salted water (some also add vinegar), in which to dip the karpas
- A white tablecloth
- A small prize (or prizes) for the finder(s) of the afikoman
- Two white candles (for the main table and each subtable)
- A jug of water, large bowl, and hand towel (to be used in the ceremonial washing of hands)
- Flowers and small vases for table decoration

For use by participants
- A copy of the order you will be using during the meal
- Wine glass/goblet
- Cup/beaker, for drinking water
- Paper napkin
- Plate
- A finger bowl of water
- Bowls/serving dishes containing the parsley, bitter herbs, sweet paste and portions of unleavened bread (either three pieces each or three at the centre, to be broken and distributed by the table 'leader')
- Bowls of salted water (how many, once again, depending on the number of those participating)
- Further plates, utensils and serving dishes, should a full shared meal be part of the proceedings
- Wine for the participants (to be poured out as appropriate by appointed table leaders)

Arranging the key elements of the meal

Place the three matzot on to the ceremonial plate, one on top of the other. Then arrange the remaining elements on the plate – beitzah (egg), pesach (shank bone), maror (bitter herb), karpas (green vegetable/herb), charoset (mixed honey, nuts, etc.), chazeret (second bitter herb). The maror, karpas, charoset and chazeret each need to be contained in a small receptacle so that they can be displayed by the leader as appropriate.

Practical points

A word concerning children

A seder meal within the Jewish tradition is essentially a family occasion, and is designed to be relaxed and informal. The search for unleavened bread and the hiding and finding of the afikoman both reflect this, each primarily designed to introduce a fun element into the proceedings and to keep children interested in what is going on. The same idea lies behind the four questions asked in a traditional meal, and taken up in *The Questioning Child* seder later in this book. Inevitably, however, children will grow restless on occasions. Obviously this needs to be kept in check so that participants can focus on what is going on, but do strive, as far as possible, to maintain an easygoing and non-religious atmosphere.

Traditionally, wine is drunk as part of the seder. If your church tradition is teetotal, you will, of course, make use of non-alcoholic wine. You may anyway wish to provide non-alcoholic wine for those who prefer this, as well as for children.

The Christian seders in this book all conclude with a celebration of the Lord's Supper, which will raise for some the question of children's participation in the Eucharist – particularly whether or not they are invited to share in the bread and wine. Each church/tradition will have their own views on this, but it is important to discuss the issue carefully prior to the event so that everyone knows where they stand on the day.

A word concerning cost

In a traditional seder, four cups of wine are drunk by each participant. For a large gathering, in particular, this will inevitably prove very costly, and, if alcoholic wine is used, it could also leave some feeling tipsy, if not drunk! For this reason, many follow the practice of participants taking just one sip from their glass as each 'cup' is announced – one glass of wine per person, in other words, suffices for the whole meal. The leader takes a sip from the main cup each time, but refills it for the next 'cup'.

A traditional seder meal – adapted, abbreviated and annotated

The following represents a simplified and abbreviated version of a Passover Haggadah. Although it includes many traditional features of a traditional seder, it is not a full or approved text. It is intended to give a flavour of the Passover meal – literally! I have assumed a relatively small gathering, and therefore indicated that the cup and various elements can be passed round. A larger group will need separate tables, each with a sub-leader and with the various elements laid on the table.

The text is annotated so that the person leading the meal can either give a brief explanation of what is going on or invite participants to read the notes as they go along. Those wishing for full Jewish texts should consult Appendix 2 at the back of the book, where details of helpful websites can be found.

Preparation

On the night of the exodus from Egypt the Israelites were ordered to make unleavened dough since there would be no time for leavened bread to rise. Since then, every practising Jewish family clears all leaven from their house prior to the start of the Festival, it being considered vital that anything containing leaven be removed before it begins. This removal would start days before the Festival and would culminate in the bedikat chametz (see page 22), which occurs the evening before the start of Passover, the entire house being searched by candlelight, room by room, for any trace of leaven. Any found would usually be destroyed. Seen as a symbol of corrupting influences, its removal is an expression both of obedience and of consecrating our lives afresh to God. So important is removing the leaven considered that, even today, all leaven in Israel is sold to a Christian cleric prior to the start of Passover, and bought back afterwards. Let all who wish to search for chametz do so now.

Before the meal, place pieces of bread around the room where the Passover meal is to take place, ensuring that these are hidden from immediate view but can swiftly be found once looked for. According to the Kabbalah (a Jewish mystical tradition), ten pieces should be hidden.

A widely followed tradition is to set an extra place at the main table, together with a poured-out cup of wine called 'the cup of Elijah'. This cup is symbolic and is not meant to be drunk by anyone. It is to symbolise both faith in the Messiah's coming and our God-given responsibility to offer hospitality to unexpected guests and those in need. Another tradition is for a child to open the door later in the service so that Elijah can 'come in'.

Search for and clearing of the leaven (*bedikat chametz*)

Begin the service by inviting young people present to search for the pieces of leavened bread. The leader collects the bread and asks a volunteer to take it out of the building and dispose of it.

Leader   Glory to you, Lord God, ruler of heaven and earth,
for your guidance concerning the eradication of leaven.

All   Glory to you, O God.

Leader   Gracious God,
remove all that is unclean from our lives
and from our world.
Cleanse us from all evil inclinations,
impure thoughts
and unworthy deeds,
and put a new heart and a right spirit within us.

All   Amen. So be it, Lord. So be it.

Lighting of Passover candles (*hadlakat ha-nerot*)

Traditionally this is carried out by a mother or grandmother, selected and primed before the service.

Mother   Glory to you, Lord God, ruler over heaven and earth,
for through your commandments you have set us apart.
Glory to you, Lord of all,
in whose name we light these candles.
Glory to you, Sovereign Lord of the universe,
giver and sustainer of life,
for once more you bring us to celebrate this feast.
May your face shine upon us.
May you sanctify us and our homes by your presence,
granting us your blessing and peace,
now and always.

All   Amen. So be it, Lord of the universe. So be it.

Blessing and sharing of first cup of wine (*kiddush/kadesh*)

A first cup of wine – the cup of sanctification and blessing – is poured.

This was drunk in celebration of God calling Israel to be his people – chosen, set apart and blessed by him – and also as a response to that calling, marking the Passover meal as a special occasion in which lives are consecrated back to God.

Leader   Glory to you, Lord God, ruler over heaven and earth,
for you have called us to be your people,
chosen by you and exalted among the nations.

All   Glory to you,
for you have given us life,
overflowing,
abundant.

Leader   Glory to you, sovereign God,
for you call us to celebrate,
remembering your faithfulness of old,
your deliverance of our forebears from oppression in Egypt.

All   Glory to you,
for your constant love
and saving power.

Leader   Glory to you, Lord of all,
for through this act of remembrance you invite us to recognise
your goodness.

All   Glory to you,
for all we celebrate now through the fruit of the vine.

The cup is passed round and all drink. Traditionally, participants drink while seated, reclining on their left side to symbolise their God-given freedom.

First hand-washing (*urechatz*)

The leader ceremonially washes his hands.

Blessing and sharing of green vegetable dipped in salty water (*karpas*)

All dip the green vegetables into salty water or vinegar.

> The green vegetables are evocative of spring, a season of hope and new beginnings, while salty water corresponds to human tears, powerfully calling to mind the sorrow and suffering of the Israelites in Egypt. The sharing of karpas, in other words, speaks of the trauma of captivity and oppression but also of the fresh start brought by God as he delivered his people from slavery.

Leader Glory to you, Lord God, ruler over heaven and earth,
for you are the creator of all.

All Glory to you,
for you bring fruit out of the earth.

All eat the karpas.

Breaking of unleavened bread (matzah) and hiding of the afikoman (*yachatz*)

> This point in the meal is marked by some of the most powerful symbolism of the whole celebration. The use of unleavened bread recalls, of course, the exodus from Egypt, prior to which the Israelites were ordered to omit leaven from the dough used in the making of bread since, such was the haste with which they would have to leave, there would be no time for this to rise. Furthermore, bread made with leaven would rapidly grow stale and mouldy in the wilderness, whereas unleavened bread kept much longer and thus, initially, would serve as some kind of provision. Known as 'the bread of the affliction', it conjures up images of the people's suffering in Egypt. It also speaks of the need to rid our lives of everything (the leaven) that corrupts and destroys, trusting and following God instead.

Leader Look and take note.
Here is the bread of suffering eaten by our fathers in Egypt.
All who are hungry,
seeking freedom from evil and slavery,
let them come now and eat,
asking that God may redeem them in turn.

All Amen, Lord, so be it.

The leader next breaks the central matzah into two pieces. The smaller piece is placed between the remaining two matzot, but the larger piece (called the afikoman) is wrapped in a napkin and passed to a helper, whose job it is to hide it somewhere in the room at an opportune moment. Young children present will be invited later to find it, the one who does so being rewarded with a small gift. (In some seders the afikoman is broken into several pieces, so that more children can search successfully. In this case a corresponding number of helpers and 'rewards' are needed rather than just the one.)

Leader Part of the unleavened bread I have broken will later be hidden somewhere in this room. Some say that hiding this piece is a reminder that God has more yet to do and reveal, but, more importantly, it is also a reminder that worship is a family occasion and should involve fun as well as more serious moments.

The leader now sets the tray to one side, and pours out a second cup of wine, participants, if appropriate, doing the same. This, however, is not yet drunk.

Telling the story *(maggid)*

At the heart of every seder meal lies the telling and retelling of the Passover story. This is done in four different ways: first, through four questions (perhaps the aspect of the meal best known to most Christians today), then through considering the attitudes of four hypothetical children, then through a potted summary of the so-called *Dayeinu* response, this meaning 'It would have been enough', and finally through explaining the significance of the key symbols displayed on the ceremonial plate.

Within the context of a Jewish family celebration, the four questions – the first of these devices – would have been put by the youngest child present. Not only does this emphasise the importance of teaching and learning about what God has done, but it also once again serves the more practical function of keeping children present feeling part of the seder and interested.

(Note that there are in fact five questions. This is because the last question, concerning reclining, was added much later, in the days of the Roman empire, the original fourth question being adapted instead into one that introduces the remainder, each of which are concerned with symbolic elements of this meal.) If the youngest child participating in the meal is unwilling or unable to participate in this way, select (in advance) the most junior child happy to do so.

Youngest child In what way does this night differ from any other?
On other nights we can eat whatever bread we like,
so why tonight must it be unleavened bread?
On other nights we can eat any herbs we wish,
so why tonight must the herbs be bitter?

On other nights we do not season the herbs,
so why tonight do we season them not once but twice?
On other nights we eat sitting down,
so why tonight do we recline instead?

Leader Let us answer your questions one by one, for it is our privilege, as well as responsibility, to answer them. First, why is this night special, different to others?

All Because today we remember how God delivered our ancestors in faith from captivity, leading them to a new life, a fresh start.

Leader Why do we eat unleavened bread tonight rather than the usual bread?

All Because on the day God delivered his people there was no time for bread to rise, so the dough was made without any kind of leaven.

Leader Why do we eat bitter herbs tonight?

All Because these remind us of the bitterness of sorrow and suffering, endured for so long by the people of Israel before God set them free.

Leader Why do we season herbs tonight, not just once but twice?

All The salty water represents the tears shed by the Israelites during their time of slavery, but the sweetness of charoset reminds us that God is able to turn those tears to laughter, our sorrow to joy.

Leader Why do we recline tonight rather than sit down to eat our food?

All This reminds us that we are no longer slaves or captives but free, set at liberty by God's grace and able, therefore, to eat and enjoy our food at leisure.

The tray is restored to its central place on the table, but the matzot are left partly covered.

Leader Our forebears became a great nation in Egypt, so that the Egyptians grew jealous, afflicting and harassing us, piling an ever-greater burden on our shoulders, until, unable to take any more, we appealed to the Lord for help. And in our suffering and sorrow he heard us, with awesome signs and wonders reaching out his hand to rescue, his mighty arm to deliver.

> We move now to the second way in which the story of the Passover is told, namely through the hypothetical cases of four children and the four attitudes they personify.

All   How, then, should we respond to a wise child, the sort who asks what God's laws and commandments mean, and why we should keep them?

Leader   You shall teach such a child enthusiastically concerning the events of the Passover and all that God has done for us.

All   And how should we respond to the disinterested child, the one who ignores or even mocks this meal, dismissively asking why we eat it?

Leader   You must emphasise all the more what God has done, and strive to bring home to the child that had the Israelites shown such an attitude, God would not have delivered them but would have left them subject to slavery.

All   What about a child unable to understand – the sort of child who struggles to grasp what this is all about?

Leader   With such a child you must keep things simple, not getting bogged down in details but highlighting the key fact that God has set us free.

All   And how, finally, should we respond to the child who, due to a lack of knowledge on the subject, feels unable even to ask a question?

Leader   In this case, patiently, sensitively and lovingly you must do your best to teach the story of God's faithfulness, doing all you can, through word and deed, to bring the child to understanding.

All   Tell us again, then, what God has done for us. Remind us once more of the story.

Leader   Indeed, let us hear it again, for however much we may understand his law, we are bound year by year to retell the story of how he set us free from captivity.

Reader 1   Following a devastating famine in Canaan, the house of Israel had journeyed to Egypt and, welcomed there by Jacob's son Joseph, had made it their home. As the years passed, so the family grew, so that in time they became a mighty family.

Reader 2   Then a new Pharaoh came to power, who knew nothing of Joseph or his family. Fear and suspicion of this immigrant population led him to oppress the Israelites, setting them to work as slaves.

Reader 3   Still, though, the people's numbers increased, until, in an act of callous genocide, Pharaoh gave orders that every first-born Israelite child should be killed. Yet, in his grace, God caused one child to be spared, his name Moses.

Reader 1   The child grew up, and heard God's call, bidding him to go to Egypt and demand that Pharaoh set his people free.

Reader 2   But Pharaoh stubbornly refused, instead increasing the workload of the Israelites until they cried out in despair. So God sent ten plagues on to the land of Egypt, until Pharaoh at last agreed to let the people go.

Reader 3   Through obedience to God's command and trust in his redeeming purpose, our children were spared and we were delivered from captivity.

All   Amen. Lord, we thank you.

The leader lifts up the second cup for all to see.

The second cup – the cup of deliverance – symbolises the joy of God's deliverance of his people from Egypt, but it is also a symbol of sorrow, for it reminds the people of Israel not just of the suffering *they* endured but of that experienced too by the Egyptians due to their stubbornness of heart. It offers a reminder, then, that so long as sorrow, evil and tragedy exist, our joy cannot be complete. The Jewish custom at this point is to dip a finger into their cups ten times and to 'spill' ten drops of wine, one for each of the plagues to afflict Egypt, these representing how joy is diminished by the suffering and sadness of others. This is the one point in a traditional seder where wine represents blood, though it does so at a symbolic level rather than in any sacrificial or redemptive sense.

The leader and participants dip a finger into their cup of wine as each plague is named, and then touch a drop on to their napkin.

Leader   Blood . . . frogs . . . lice . . . disease among cattle . . . pestilence . . . boils . . . hailstones . . . locusts . . . darkness . . . death of the first-born . . .

The leader and participants put their cup of wine down, without drinking.

Next comes the third way of telling the story, using the response *Dayeinu* (meaning 'That alone would have been enough for us' *or* 'It would have been enough').

Leader Remember how richly God has blessed us, how much he has done.
If he had merely rescued us out of the hands of the Egyptians
and not revealed the impotence of their idols . . .

All *Dayeinu*

Leader If he had merely exposed their gods as worthless
and not sent us out loaded with treasures . . .

All *Dayeinu*

Leader If he had merely led us empty-handed into the wilderness
and not seen us any further . . .

All *Dayeinu*

Leader If he had merely parted the waters of the sea
and not let us walk across . . .

All *Dayeinu*

Leader If he had merely led us safely through to the other side
and not obstructed the Egyptians . . .

All *Dayeinu*

Leader If he had merely destroyed those who sought to take our lives
and not offered further assistance . . .

All *Dayeinu*

Leader If he had merely supplied our needs during the long years
in the desert
and not provided divine sustenance . . .

All *Dayeinu*

Leader If he had merely given us bread from heaven
and not given us his law . . .

All *Dayeinu*

Leader If he had merely given us his commandments on Mount Sinai and not taken any more interest in our welfare . . .

All *Dayeinu*

Leader Yet God did all this and so much more,
blessing us beyond words.

All For his great goodness, we praise him.

Next comes the final means of telling the story, through explaining the meaning of the key symbols displayed on the ceremonial plate.

Leader Tradition tells us that if we fail to explain the meaning of the elements of the Passover, then we are failing in our duty and not properly celebrating the feast.

The matzot is uncovered.

The leader takes the pesach from the ceremonial plate and holds it up for all to see.

Leader This represents the Passover lamb, its blood daubed by the Israelites over their doorposts in obedience to God's command. Doing this served as a sign to the avenging angel to pass over their homes and leave their first-born untouched.

All For your grace, Lord, we thank you.

The leader takes the beitzah from the ceremonial plate and again holds it up for all to see.

Leader This symbolises distress and despair, but also new beginnings. Having been roasted in fire, it represents all those who have faced the ordeal of grief and mourning, offering a reminder, then, of the suffering and sorrow in our world. But eggs also are traditionally a symbol of new life. So we are reminded also that God offers new life to us and to all.

All For your renewing power, Lord, we thank you.

The leader raises the first matzah.

All What does matzah signify? Why do we eat it?

Leader It recalls the bread of affliction taken by our fathers as they left Egypt. As the Scripture (Exodus 12:39) puts it: 'They used the dough they had brought from Egypt to bake unleavened bread; unleavened because there had been insufficient time to add yeast when they fled from Egypt, or to prepare any other provisions.'

The leader puts down the matzah and lifts up the maror (mixed with chazeret, if used).

All What does maror signify? Why do we eat it?

Leader It means bitter herb and recalls the bitterness caused to our forebears by the Egyptians. As the Scripture (Exodus 1:13, 14) puts it: 'The Egyptians ruthlessly imposed ever more demanding tasks upon the Israelites, forcing them to make bricks and work the fields, their lives made bitter by hard labour.'

The leader puts down the maror, covers the matzah, and lifts up the second cup of wine.

Leader It is our joy and privilege to acknowledge and acclaim the Lord our God.

All Glory to you, Lord God, ruler over heaven and earth,
for though once we were slaves, now we are free.

All drink the second cup of wine, reclining as they do so.

Second hand-washing and blessing (rachtzah)

The leader and all those present ceremonially wash their hands in preparation for eating.

Leader Glory to you, Lord God, ruler over heaven and earth,
for all the commandments through which you consecrate us
to your service,
and for your instruction to wash and be clean.

The leader picks up the matzot from the ceremonial plate, placing the broken piece between the two whole portions.

Leader Glory to you, Lord God, ruler over all,
for you bring bread from the earth.

The leader lifts up the two whole matzot.

Leader Glory to you, Lord God, ruler over heaven and earth,
for all the commandments through which you consecrate us to
your service,
and especially for your instructions concerning the matzah.

The leader breaks the whole matzot into pieces, and hands these out.
Participants retain the bread in their hands until all are served.

All Glory to you, Lord God, ruler over heaven and earth,
for providing bread and nourishment.

All eat.

Eating of the bitter herbs *(maror – and chazeret, if used)*

Leader As the Scripture instructs us, as well as bread we eat bitter herbs.

All dip the maror into the charoset, immediately shaking the charoset off
so that its sweetness cannot hide the bitterness of the maror.

All Glory to you, sovereign God,
for this maror,
and all it signifies.

All eat the maror.

Eating of maror and matzah *(korech)* – The Hillel sandwich

The leader breaks the remaining half of matzot into two, and places
bitter herbs and charoset between these. Participants make a similar
'sandwich'.

The charoset represents the clay and straw that the Israelites had to use in
Egypt to make bricks and mortar, but its sweetness once again speaks of
God, and the way hope in his purpose gave them strength even in suffering.

Leader As it is written: 'They shall eat the pesach with matzah and bitter
herbs.'

All eat, while reclining.

The festival meal *(shulchan orech)*

At this point other food may be shared as a communal meal. Otherwise, a hymn or song may be sung at this point.

Drinking of third cup of wine *(barech)*

The leader pours out the third cup of wine – the cup of redemption – and blesses it.

This third cup celebrates God's deliverance of his people both from the plague of death and from captivity.

Leader   Glory to you, Lord God, ruler over heaven and earth,
for you have delivered us
just as you delivered your people of old,
bringing us to share in this special moment,
as generations have shared before us.
Your will be done,
your kingdom come.

All   Glory to you, Lord God, ruler over heaven and earth,
for you have created the fruit of the vine.

Leader   May the God of mercy rule over us,
now and always.

All   Amen, so be it.

Leader   May the God of grace bless and keep us,
now and for evermore.

All   Amen, so be it.

Leader   May the God of love guide our footsteps,
this and every day.

All   Amen, so be it.

Leader   May the God of all creation grant us our daily bread,
satisfy our need,
and grant us his peace.

All   Amen.

All drink the third cup of wine.

Drinking of fourth cup of wine and completion of Passover celebration *(nirtzah)*

> *The leader pours a fourth cup of wine, the cup of thanksgiving and hope.*

Leader   Glory to you, Lord of all,
for you have created the fruit of the vine.

All   Glory to you, Lord,
glory and praise to you.
Amen.

> *At this point a hallel psalm is sung or said. Psalm 136 is often used, but the Passover hallels also include Psalms 113 to 118. Below is an adaptation of verses from various psalms.*

Leader   Let us, then, offer a song of worship.

All   Do not give glory to us, O Lord;
it belongs not to us but to you,
for you are faithful in all things and constant in love.

Leader   Praise the Lord. Let all his servants praise and extol him.

All   May the Lord's name be exalted,
today and every day,
now and always.

Leader   He reigns supreme over the nations,
and his glory fills the universe.

All   Who can compare to the One who rules on high,
before all,
above all,
beyond all?

Leader   He lifts up the poor and needy from the scrap heap,
giving them the honour accorded to royalty.

All   How awesome is the love he unfailingly shows us;
his faithfulness never ends.

Leader   In our distress we cried out for help,
and he came and rescued us.

All   If God is with us, what shall we ever fear?
What can anyone ultimately do to us?

Leader   You are our God, O Lord,
and we will give you thanks.

All   You are our God,
and we will praise you.

Leader   The stone that the builders rejected has become the keystone,
the cornerstone on which all else is built.

All   God has done this,
and it is wonderful to behold.

Leader   This is the day that God has given.

All   We will rejoice and be glad in it.

Leader   Praise the Lord!

All   Amen. Praise the Lord!
(Adapted from Psalm 115:1; 113:1-8; 117:2; 118:5-6; 119:28; 119:22-24; 117:2b)

A song or hymn of praise may be sung at this point.

The fourth cup of wine is drunk.

Leader   Glory to you, Lord,
for you have blessed us and satisfied our needs.

All   Glory to you, Lord,
for you have shown us mercy and called us to be your people.

Leader   Glory to you, Lord,
for this great festival of celebration.

All   Glory to you, Lord,
for giving us our inheritance.

Leader   Glory to you, Lord,
for you are good in all you do.

All   Glory to you, Lord,
now and always.

It is customary for participants to end the seder by saying together the words:

'Next year, in Jerusalem!'

A Christian seder meal (1)
The paschal lamb

This seder represents an adaptation of the Passover Haggadah in which a Christian element is interwoven with the original. It follows an abbreviated version of the traditional seder pattern, but moves on to develop this in terms of the gospel and, in particular, the celebration of the Lord's Supper.

Preparation

When setting up the tables, prepare an extra place at the head table, and include a poured-out cup of wine – 'the cup of Elijah'. This picks up an ancient Jewish tradition, Elijah being the one many expected to announce the arrival of the Messiah. The cup, which no one drinks from, symbolises both expectation of the Messiah's coming and a willingness to offer hospitality to unexpected guests and those in need. Another tradition is for a child to open the door later in the service so that Elijah can come in.

Before the meal, place pieces of bread around the room where the Passover meal is to take place, ensuring that these are hidden from immediate view but can swiftly be found once looked for. According to the Kabbalah (a Jewish mystical tradition), ten pieces should be hidden.

Welcome and introduction

Leader Welcome to this celebration of what we have termed 'a Christian seder'. You may be wondering what we mean by this, so let me explain. A seder meal can perhaps be described best as a cross between an order of service and a menu, the word 'seder' referring to the pattern used for centuries by Jews across the world as they celebrate the Passover meal. This is not to say there is only one form of words to be used during the meal; far from it – the Passover tradition is a living and dynamic one that encourages innovation and creativity.

We are not, though, going to share today in a Passover meal; ours instead is to be an interpretation of that in the light of Christ, adapted in the context of our faith and reflecting the convictions we hold dear, but recognising our shared roots and so much we hold in common with the Jewish community, including worshipping the same God. Jesus himself, of course, was born and raised as a Jew, schooled in the law and the prophets. Jesus saw himself and was seen by his followers as fulfilling God's promise to rescue and redeem his people through his chosen deliverer. So much in Jesus' life and teaching, including, of course, the Last Supper, reflect that background, and through understanding more of what that means our faith can only be deepened and enriched. This evening, then, as we share in this seder meal, we will explore what God's gracious dealings, revealed in both the Old Testament and the New, have to say to us today in our journey of discipleship.

We start, though, with a tradition associated with Passover: the search for and disposing of leavened bread, called 'chametz' in Hebrew. As well as having a spiritual meaning this introduces us to a very practical aspect of the seder; namely that, for the Jews it is a family occasion, involving children as much as adults and making room for their sense of fun coupled with their youthful enthusiasm and eagerness to learn. Leaven, in Jewish tradition, was seen as the cause of decay and putrefaction, and thus as a symbol of everything that brings corruption and sinfulness into our lives. The people of Israel, on the night of the exodus from Egypt, were ordered to dispose of anything containing leaven, taking with them only unleavened dough. The significance of this is obvious: they were about to begin a new life, set free from the old by God. Since then, every practising Jewish family clears all leaven from their house prior to the start of the Festival, it being considered vital to remove anything containing leaven by that time. This removal would start days before the Festival and would culminate in the *bedikat chametz* (see below) which occurs the evening before the start of Passover, the entire house being searched by candlelight, room by room, for any trace of leaven. Any found would usually be destroyed. Its removal is an expression both of obedience and of consecrating our lives afresh to God. So important is removing the leaven considered that, even today, all leaven in Israel is sold to a Christian cleric prior to the start of Passover, and bought back afterwards. Let all who wish to search for chametz do so now.

Young people present search for the pieces of leavened bread. The leader collects the bread and asks a helper to take it out of the room.

Leader Gracious God,
we worship and acclaim you,
for you lead us into new life,
setting us free from everything that destroys,

that estranges us from you and one another,
that prevents us from being the people you would have us be.
Though we continue to fail you in so much,
you are constantly at work,
making of us a new creation.

All Sovereign God,
for your great goodness and awesome mercy,
we praise and thank you.

Leader Lord,
take away everything that is unfaithful in our lives.
Cleanse us from all evil inclinations,
impure thoughts
and unworthy deeds,
and put a new heart and a right spirit within us.

All Amen. So be it.

Lighting of Passover candles

Traditionally, this is undertaken by a mother or grandmother (who should be selected and primed before the service).

Leader We come now to the lighting of Passover candles,
symbols of God's love shining into our world
and illuminating our hearts.
I have asked (*name*), as a representative of motherhood,
to light the candles for us this evening.

The candles are lit.

Mother Glory to you, sovereign Lord of the universe,
for you have set us apart by your grace.
Once we were no people,
but you have called us to know and love you.
In your name we light these candles,
acknowledging you as the giver and sustainer of life.

All May your face shine upon us.
Sanctify our homes, our lives and our world by your presence,
and grant us your blessing and peace,
now and always.

Blessing and sharing of first cup of wine

A first cup of wine is poured.

Leader   In a traditional seder, four cups of wine are drunk, the first called the cup of sanctification and blessing. For the people of Israel it speaks of God's grace in calling them to be his people and rescuing them from all that held them captive. For us as Christians it speaks also of God calling us, setting us apart in turn, and redeeming us through the sacrificial self-offering of Christ.

All   Glory to you, Lord of all,
for your mighty acts in creation and across history.

Leader   You are a chosen race,
a royal priesthood,
a holy nation,
a people whom God has set apart,
so that you may declare the goodness of him who called you
out of darkness
into his wonderful light.
Once, you were not a people –
now you are the people of God;
once you had not obtained forgiveness –
now you have received mercy.

(1 Peter 2:9-10)

All   Glory to you, Lord God,
for you have called us to know and love you.

Leader   Glory to you, Lord, for your great faithfulness and saving power.

All   Glory to you, sovereign God,
for this act of commemoration through which you invite us
to recognise your goodness.

The cup is passed round and all drink. Traditionally, participants recline on their left side to symbolise their God-given freedom.

Blessing and sharing of green vegetable dipped in salty water

The leader holds up a sprig of parsley and a bowl of salty water.

Leader   We come now to the eating of green vegetable, traditionally parsley, dipped into salty water. Green is symbolic of springtime, and reminds us of the renewing power of God, experienced in new birth, new beginnings, new life. Alongside that promise of springtime, the salty water offers another symbol, recalling the tears shed by the people of Israel as they suffered in Egypt – tears of pain, sorrow and despair. We are reminded, then, that alongside joy, life brings sadness, alongside spring, winter.

All take some parsley, dip it into the salty water, and eat it.

Leader Glory to you, Lord God, ruler over heaven and earth,
for, whatever life brings, you are with us.

All In joy or sorrow,
pleasure or pain,
you are there,
striving to fulfil your loving purpose.
Glory to you, O God.

Breaking of unleavened bread

Leader The next part of our traditional seder meal makes use of another symbol – unleavened bread, *matzot* or 'the bread of the affliction'. It recalls the time when the people of Israel waited in Egypt for their deliverance, instructed to eat their meal with unleavened bread since there would be no time for bread made with leaven to rise.

The leader uncovers the pieces of bread, holds up the middle one, and breaks it into two pieces, setting aside the largest piece to serve as the afikoman and placing the smaller piece between the remaining pieces of bread. The leader then lifts up the tray bearing the bread.

Leader For us as Christians this calls to mind words from the New Testament:

Jesus suffered outside the gate of Jerusalem, sanctifying the people through his blood. Get rid of the old yeast, so that you may become a fresh consignment, truly unleavened. For Jesus has been sacrificed as our Passover lamb. So, then, let us celebrate the festival, not with the old form of leaven, the yeast of enmity and immorality that marked our former way of life, but with the unleavened bread of sincerity and truth.

(Hebrews 13:12; 1 Corinthians 5:7-8)

All   Amen.

The leader pours out a second cup of wine, participants, if appropriate, doing the same. This, however, is not yet drunk.

Telling the story

Leader   Central to any seder meal is the telling and retelling of the Passover story. In a Jewish Passover this is done in four different ways: through the so-called four questions, the four attitudes, the *dayeinu* response and the k'arah symbols. The four questions in the context of a Jewish family celebration would be put by the youngest child present, partly to emphasise the importance of teaching and learning about what God has done, but mainly simply to engage the interest of young people present. The four attitudes pick up the different attitudes people may have not just to Passover but to faith in general. The *dayeinu* response gives an opportunity to emphasise the innumerable ways in which God shows his blessing. Finally the explanation of the k'arah symbols affords the opportunity to reflect at greater depth on central aspects of the Passover story. To make use of each of these teaching devices would take too long for a service such as this, so instead we simply listen now to a summary of that story.

Reader 1   Sold into slavery by his brothers, Joseph rose, by God's grace, to become Pharaoh's foremost official.

Reader 2   When a catastrophic famine arose in Canaan, Joseph's father Jacob and his remaining sons set out for Egypt to buy food, finally being reunited and reconciled with Joseph.

Reader 3   They settled down in the land, multiplying and prospering to the point that, when a new Pharaoh replaced the old, they became seen as foes rather than friends, an enemy within.

Reader 1   So began an episode of ever-increasing oppression – the Hebrews being set to work as slaves, labouring in the construction of Egypt's mighty buildings.

Reader 2   Worse was to follow when Pharaoh gave the brutal order that all first-born sons of the Israelites should be killed. It was a time of abject despair and untold suffering in which faith, understandably, was tested to the limit, the people's cry for help seemingly ignored.

Reader 3 One child, however, had escaped the slaughter – the boy Moses. Set adrift in a wicker basket by his devoted mother and subsequently found by Pharaoh's daughter among the bulrushes, he was raised in Pharaoh's household, reared there by his own mother, who was employed to nurse him.

Reader 1 His mother left Moses in no doubt as to his true heritage, and in a fit of temper as a young man, he struck and killed an Egyptian whom he discovered beating a Hebrew slave, being forced, as a result, to flee for his life into Midian.

Reader 2 While he was working in Midian as a shepherd for his father-in-law Jethro, there came a moment that was to change not just Moses' life but that also of his fellow-Israelites and, indeed, just about every Jew since, for, sensing God's presence in a burning bush, he received a call to return to Egypt and demand that Pharaoh release his people.

Reader 3 It was not a call he relished, far from it; indeed, the prospect was so terrifying that he did all he could to wriggle off the hook, only finally agreeing to go if his brother Aaron could accompany him.

Reader 1 The response of Pharaoh was all too predictable – a blanket refusal – and so began a series of ten plagues sent by God, designed to break the spirit of the Egyptians until Pharaoh had no option but to give way.

Reader 2 The last plague, in a tragic irony, was to be the death of the Egyptian first-born, Pharaoh's order to slaughter the first-born sons of the Israelites returning to haunt him.

Reader 3 Before this last plague God commanded the Israelites to slaughter a lamb, daubing its blood on the lintels of their homes. Thus his agent of death would know to *pass over* their houses.

Reader 1 The carnage among the Egyptians that night was to be the final straw, Pharaoh not just allowing but ordering the Israelites to leave, and heaping gold and jewellery upon them as a final incentive.

Reader 2 A new chapter for the people had started – they were free!

Reader 3 Yes, there were still to be testing moments to come, not least when Pharaoh changed his mind and sent an army to pursue them, but through it all Moses remained faithful, leading the people through the Red Sea, and then on through long years in the wilderness until, at last, they entered God's Promised Land, a land flowing with milk and honey.

All Amen. Lord, we thank you.

The leader picks up the second cup of wine and holds it up for all to see.

Leader This second cup – the cup of deliverance – serves in a traditional seder meal as a symbol of joy, recalling God's deliverance of his people. At the same time, it also symbolises sorrow, for before drinking it participants in the meal dip their fingers into the wine and spill ten drops on to their napkins, one for each of the ten plagues.

Here, then, is a reminder of suffering and evil brought into the world by human sinfulness, these still so much a part of our world today. It offers evocative expression to the fact that, as long as heartache and heartbreak continue, our joy cannot be complete, for it is necessarily diminished by the suffering and sadness of others.

This, then, is a fitting moment to pause and pray for others, thinking of those places in our world today still afflicted by hatred and bloodshed, and of individuals known to us enduring sorrow.

All Loving God,
reach out into the hurt and pain of our world,
the injustice, hunger and hatred,
the sorrow and suffering
and bring your strength,
help,
deliverance
and new beginnings.
Amen.

Leader It is our joy and privilege tonight to acclaim the Lord our God,
for he has transformed imprisonment to liberty,
tears to laughter,
despair to celebration
and darkness to light.

All Glory to you, Lord God, sovereign over all,
for though once we were slaves, now we are free.

All drink the second cup of wine, reclining as they do so.

The leader then takes the shank bone from the ceremonial plate and holds it up for all to see.

Leader This represents the Passover lamb, a reminder of the lambs sacrificed in Egypt in obedience to God's commands, thus indicating to the avenging angel that it should pass over the homes of the Israelites.

For us as Christians the Passover lamb takes on new significance in Christ, the one whose blood was shed to bring us freedom and new life. We see in him the definitive sacrifice, offered so that we might also become his people, chosen and precious to him.

All For your grace, Lord, we praise you.

Leader 'Look!' said John, as Jesus approached.
'This is the Lamb of God, who comes to take away the sin of the world.'

All For your grace, Lord, we thank you.

Leader You have been redeemed from misguided ways of the past,
not with silver or gold, the value of which fades,
but through the priceless blood of Christ –
a perfect lamb without any kind of flaw or fault.

(1 Peter 1:18, 19)

All For your grace, Lord, we worship you.

The leader uncovers and lifts up the broken piece of unleavened bread for all to see.

Leader As we have been reminded, this represents unleavened bread hurriedly snatched by the Israelites as they fled from Egypt. As the Scripture (Exodus 12:39) puts it: 'They used the dough they had brought from Egypt to bake unleavened bread; unleavened because there was insufficient time for yeast to rise before they were driven out of Egypt, or to prepare any other provisions.'

All Glory to you, Lord God, ruler over heaven and earth,
for providing bread and nourishment.

The leader breaks the unleavened bread into pieces, and distributes these. Participants retain the bread in their hands until all are served.

All eat.

Eating of the bitter herbs

The leader holds up the bitter herbs (parsley).

Leader This represents the bitterness of life endured by the people of Israel under Egyptian oppression.

As the Scripture (Exodus 1:13, 14) puts it: 'The Egyptians ruthlessly imposed ever more demanding tasks upon the Israelites, forcing them to make bricks and work the fields, their lives made bitter by hard labour.'

As the Scripture instructs us, alongside bread we eat bitter herbs.

All dip the bitter herbs into the sweet paste, immediately shaking off any residue so that its sweetness cannot hide the bitterness of the herbs.

Leader May the taste of these herbs help us to empathise with those whose lot is still bitter to endure, and to reach out in love towards them.

All Speak, Lord,
and help us to respond.

All eat the bitter herbs.

Eating of bitter herb and unleavened bread sandwich

The leader holds up another sprig of parsley.

Leader These represent the bitterness we have already spoken of, but also the sweetness of God's goodness in bringing joy out of sorrow, freedom out of captivity, and hope out of despair.

The leader takes the remaining portion of unleavened bread and breaks it in two, putting a little bitter herb on one half and placing this back on the ceremonial plate. The leader then holds up the bowl of sweet paste.

Leader This mixture represents the clay and straw used by the Hebrews in Egypt to make bricks and mortar, but it reminds us also of the sweetness of hope in God, hope realised as he set them free from slavery.

All Glory to you, sovereign God.

All take some bread, break it in two, dip herbs into the sweet paste, place these on top of one piece of the bread, and then place the other piece of bread on top again to make a sandwich.

Leader   As it is written:
'They shall eat unleavened bread and bitter herbs.'

All   We eat, Lord, with thanksgiving.

All eat, while reclining.

At this point other food may be shared as a communal meal, boiled eggs often being eaten as the first course. Otherwise (or after the full meal) the seder continues as follows.

Drinking of the third cup of wine

Leader   We fill now a third cup, the cup of redemption, through which the people of Israel celebrate how, through their obedience to his command, God delivered them both from the plague of death and from captivity.

The leader pours out the third cup of wine.

Leader   Hear the word of the Lord.

Reader   We have all gone astray like sheep,
each going our own way,
but the Lord has laid on him the offences of us all.
He was broken and afflicted,
yet his mouth remained closed.
Though he was led like a lamb to the slaughter,
he was silent;
like a lamb before its shearers he did not open his mouth.
He poured out his life,
being counted in death among sinners,
yet the reality is that he took upon himself the sins of many,
 interceding on behalf of wrongdoers.

(Isaiah 53:6, 7, 12b)

Leader   Glory to you, living God,
for this cup celebrating the deliverance of your people.

Leader   Let go, then, of guilt,
put aside despair,
move on and embrace the future,
for God has set us free.

All   The past is dealt with,
our mistakes blotted out,
wiped away.

Leader   Today,
here and now,
God offers us a fresh start,
new beginnings.

All   No more slavery to self,
hostages to fortune.
The price has been paid,
the sacrifice offered,
redemption and new life are ours through Jesus Christ.

Leader   Reach out in joy and wonder
and receive all that God has given.

All   Amen.

All drink the third cup of wine.

Leader   May the God of love guide our footsteps in the way of peace,
this and every day.

All   Amen, so be it.

The Hallel Psalm

Leader   Let us, then, offer God our worship.

All   Do not give glory to us, O Lord;
it belongs not to us but to you,
for you are faithful in all things
and constant in love.

Leader   Praise the Lord.
Let all his servants praise and extol him.

All   May the Lord's name be exalted,
today and every day,
now and always.

Leader He reigns supreme over the nations,
and his glory fills the universe.

All Who can compare to the One who rules on high,
before all,
above all,
beyond all?

Leader He lifts up the poor and needy from the scrap heap,
giving them the honour accorded to royalty.

All How awesome is the love he unfailingly shows us;
his faithfulness never ends.

Leader In our distress we cried out for help,
and he came and rescued us.

All If God is with us, what shall we ever fear?
What can anyone ultimately do to us?

Leader You are our God, O Lord,
and we will give you thanks.

All You are our God,
and we will praise you.

Leader The stone that the builders rejected
has become the keystone,
the cornerstone on which all else is built.

All God has done this,
and it is wonderful to behold.

Leader This is the day that God has given.

All We will rejoice and be glad in it.

Leader Praise the Lord!

All Amen. Praise the Lord!
(Adapted from Psalm 115:1; 113:1-8; 117:2; 118:5, 6; 119:28; 119:22-24; 117:2b)

A song or hymn of praise may be sung at this point.

The fourth cup of wine

The leader pours out a fourth cup of wine.

Leader   The fourth cup of wine drunk at a traditional seder symbolises thanksgiving and hope. It is a reminder of all God has done, and of all he will yet do.

All   Glory to you, Lord.
Glory and praise to you.
Amen.

All drink.

The Lord's Supper

Leader   A traditional Jewish Passover meal would now be nearly at an end, but in our case the meal is very much incomplete, for we see the Passover as pointing beyond itself, finding new fulfilment and meaning in Christ. We do so at his instigation, Jesus having expressly chosen this festival to coincide with his suffering and death. As the Scriptures tell us: 'On the opening day of the feast of unleavened bread, Jesus' disciples approached him and asked, "Where should we get things ready for us to share Passover together?"' He answered, "Go to a certain man in the city, and pass on this message: 'The teacher's says that the appointed time is near; I will therefore observe the Passover with my disciples, in your house.'" They did as instructed, and made ready the Passover meal.'

Helpers bring bread and wine to the table. Wafers can, of course, be used if preferred, but the symbolism of a loaf of bread at this point is much more powerful.

Leader   Before breaking bread at Passover it was customary to wash one's hands, thus ensuring ritual purity. Before he broke bread, Jesus went one step further, washing not hands but feet, and not his own but those of Peter, the man he knew would three times deny him. In this demonstration of humility we see the one who came to serve, to offer his life, to put others before himself; the one who makes *us* clean too, not on the outside but deep within – remade, renewed!

At this point the leader may symbolically wash a volunteer's feet (leaders at tables may do likewise).

All Lord,
we too have made ready to share with you.

Leader Jesus said to them, 'I am the bread of life; no one who comes to me will ever hunger, and whoever trusts in me will never thirst. The Father's will is this: that all those who see and believe in the Son will enjoy eternal life, for I will raise them up on the last day.'

The leader holds up the bread for all to see.

Leader Taking some bread, and thanking God for it, he broke it into pieces and distributed it among them, saying, 'This is my body, given for you; do this, to remember me.'

All Lord, we remember.

The leader puts down the bread and pours wine into a chalice (filling a second chalice or more if necessary). The leader then holds up the chalice for all to see.

Leader Similarly, taking a cup after supper, he said, 'This cup, poured out for you, represents the new covenant, sealed by my blood.'

All Lord, we praise you.

Leader Let us thank God for the bread we will share.

All Amen.

Leader Glory to you, Lord of all,
for you give us daily bread,
living bread, food to nurture body and soul.

All Glory, honour and praise to you
for *this* bread, and all it means.

Leader Let us give thanks for the wine we will share.

All Amen.

Leader Glory to you, Lord of all,
for you meet our thirst,
giving us wine to celebrate,
new wine,
everlasting wine.

All   Glory to you, Lord,
for giving this wine, and all it means.

The leader puts down the chalice and picks up the loaf of bread, breaking it into four chunks.

Leader   Broken bread,
Christ's body,
offered freely,
without reserve –
a sacrifice of love.

All   For your awesome grace, Lord,
we thank you.

The leader places the chunks of bread on to serving plates, and hands these to servers to distribute among the participants. Participants stay seated, breaking off a morsel of bread and retaining it until all are served.

Leader   Eat this bread
and let God's love fill you,
allaying your hunger and nourishing your soul.
Eat,
and be filled.

All eat the bread.

The leader lifts up the chalice for all to see.

Leader   Poured-out wine,
Christ's blood,
offered gladly,
without condition –
a gift beyond price.

All   For your awesome love, Lord,
we thank you.

The leader hands the chalice(s) to a helper(s) to serve participants.

Leader   Drink this wine
and let his grace engulf you,
quenching your thirst and refreshing your spirit.

Drink,
and be satisfied.

All drink.

Leader Speak, Lord, through the awfulness yet awesomeness
of this meal.
Speak of the Christ who was beaten, bruised and broken for us,
who suffered darkness and death for us,
who offers light and life *to* us.

All You have spoken, Lord.
We thank you.

Leader Remind us, sovereign God,
in this world of so much sorrow, pain, evil and hurt,
of the ultimate triumph of your love,
the victory you have won in Christ over hatred,
intolerance and oppression,
over all that holds us captive and denies us life.

All Teach us that, however strong evil may seem,
however entrenched it may appear in our world,
your gracious purpose will finally win through.
Amen.

Leader We have eaten together a seder meal,
remembering through bread and wine
God's deliverance from slavery in Egypt.

All Worthy is the Lamb that was slain
to receive power and riches, wisdom and strength.

Leader We have shared together the Lord's Supper,
celebrating how Christ has set us free
from *everything* and *anything* that holds us captive.

All Worthy is the Lamb that was slain
to receive honour and glory and blessing.

Leader We have eaten,
but the meal is not ended,
for Jesus goes on feeding us day after day,
through living bread and water,
food that nourishes us deep within.

All   So then, we go on our way, resolved to celebrate every moment
he gives us,
living each to the full,
until that day dawns when we will enter his Father's kingdom,
and feast with him for all eternity.

Leader   Let us go in peace
to love and serve the Lord.

All   Amen.

A Christian seder meal (2)
The questioning child

This abbreviated Christian seder makes use of the celebrated question-and-answer device to explore once again the links between the Passover and the Lord's Supper. Normally four questions would be put by the youngest child present, but this service broadens both the number of questions asked and the number of children doing the asking. The position of certain elements of the seder has been shifted to accommodate this. Telling the Passover story features much more prominently, instead of coming during the middle of the meal. Ensure that participating children are primed in advance and given time to practise. It may also be worth asking a few of the older children to be ready to step in should younger questioners dry up with last-minute nerves.

As well as being an act of worship this seder is a useful teaching tool, reminding participants of our Christian (and Jewish) heritage and of the meaning of the Eucharist.

Welcome and introduction

Leader Welcome to our seder meal, a meal in which we are going to explore two sacred traditions: the Passover festival of the Jews and the Christian sacrament of the Lord's Supper. The first, of course, is not *our* tradition, and so what we are going to share in today is not a Passover meal in the strict sense of the word but a re-enactment of certain symbolic features prominent within Passover, the meaning of each explained as we eat and drink. The Jewish word seder means, simply, order, and the text (or haggadah) we will follow today, though making use of the order customarily followed at Passover, is finally an interpretation of this in the context of Christ, adapted in the light of faith and reflecting our Christian convictions.

Do not imagine, however, that there is one authoritative form of the Passover meal that we are diverging from. Nothing could be further from the truth. It is estimated that there are around 2,000 versions of this most ancient of Jewish feasts, the tradition being a vigorous and vibrant one in which originality and inventiveness is not just accepted but encouraged. Although we see the meal as finding ultimate fulfilment in Christ, do not assume this means dismissing past insights and understandings. Our faith emerged from the seedbed of Judaism and holds much in common with it, the God we worship being the same, even though our understandings of his saving activity may differ. The people of Israel have always had, and continue to have, a special place in God's heart, and their long history of faith despite unimaginable suffering and persecution should similarly command respect in our hearts today.

Jesus himself, of course, as a Jew would have celebrated Passover many times, and it is to him that we owe the idea of a Christian seder, for it was precisely this that he instituted during the Passover festival in the meal we know as the Lord's Supper. The time he chose, the meal he shared, the words he used, and the events that followed leave us in no doubt that he intended us to understand his life and ministry, and in particular his death, in terms of the Passover, his suffering and sacrifice giving the powerful symbolism of the festival new and yet more redolent meaning. This evening, then, our seder meal will include not only elements of Passover but also a simple celebration of the Eucharist, the first leading on to the second.

Central to any seder meal is the telling and retelling of the Passover story. In a Jewish Passover this is traditionally done four times, but tonight we tell the story just once, using perhaps the best-known aspect of the traditional meal: the question-and-answer device. Within the context of a Jewish family celebration, four key questions would be put by the youngest child present, these emphasising the importance of both teaching and learning about what God has done. Usually, these would be asked and then answered together, but in this seder we have included many other questions, interspersing them throughout the course of our meal in order to explain each aspect of what is going on. Instead of just one child putting the questions, they will be put by a number of our young people.

Young people also feature in the first part of our celebration: the search for and disposing of leavened bread, called 'chametz' in Hebrew. A traditional Jewish custom, this would usually take place well before the Festival; any suggestion of beginning the meal with leaven still around would be unthinkable to a practising Jew. Around the room pieces of bread have been hidden. Can any of the children or young people here this evening find them?

Young people search for the pieces of leavened bread. The leader collects the bread and asks a helper to dispose of it, ensuring it is taken out of the room.

Child What was that all about? It was fun, but what does it mean?

Leader The Jewish Law commands that all food containing leaven – which includes bread – be removed from Jewish homes before Passover. Partly this recalls how, when they left Egypt, there was no time to wait for leavened dough to rise. Partly, it speaks of the need to rid our lives of all corrupting influences, leaven being seen as that which causes food to go mouldy and rot. Every practising Jewish family, therefore, clears all leaven from their house prior to the start of the Festival. This removal would start days before-hand and would culminate in a fun ceremony rather like that we've just shared in. The entire house would be searched by candle-light, room by room, for any trace of leaven, and any found would be destroyed.

All Come, then, Lord,
and purge us of everything that is unworthy in our lives.

Leader Lord of all,
for setting us free from everything that estranges us from you and one another,
preventing us from being the people you would have us be,
we praise you.

All For redeeming and restoring us despite our repeated failure,
making of us a new creation,
we praise you.

Leader Cleanse us from all faithless desires, thoughts and deeds,
and put a new heart and a right spirit within us.

All Lord, hear us. Amen.

Lighting of Passover candles

Leader Integral to every seder celebration is the lighting of candles.

Child Is this simply to give us light?

Leader That's certainly part of the reason. Traditionally two candles are lit at every table, these symbolising both light and joy. They remind us of God's love shining into our world and illuminating our hearts. Some also say that the candles stand for two key words associated with the Ten Commandments: 'remember' and 'keep'.

Child   So who's going to light the candles? Can *I* do it?

Leader   I know you'd like to, but the custom in a seder meal is for a mother or grandmother to light the candles.

Child   Why are these chosen?

Leader   Because it is the mother who sets the foundation of every Jewish home. Without all she does, we would not be able to celebrate this meal. I've asked (*name*), then, as a representative of motherhood, to light the candles for us this evening.

The candles are lit.

Mother   Lord of all,
in celebration of your loving purpose that has called us here,
setting us apart as your people,
not by any merit of our own but by your grace,
we light now these candles.
Shine in our hearts,
and through our lives,
bringing glory to your name.
Amen.

All   Shine upon us, our homes, our loved ones and our world,
by your presence granting to all your blessing and peace,
now and always.

A song or hymn of praise may be sung at this point.

Child   In what way does this night differ from any other?

Leader   A good question and one we do well to consider. Tonight differs from others because it is a sacred festival, reminding us of how God delivered our ancestors in faith from captivity, leading them to a new life, a fresh start.

Child   So where were they held captive?

Leader   For many years, after first having settled and multiplied in Egypt, they were forced to work as slaves, making bricks and building towns and cities. They were cruelly treated, life so hard for them that they cried out in despair.

Child   And what happened then?

Leader   God heard their cry and sent Moses, who, as a child, had escaped Pharaoh's slaughter of Israelite newborn boys. Moses went to Egypt and demanded that his people be set free.

Child   What did Pharaoh say to that?

Leader   He not only refused, but also increased the workload of the Israelites, so God sent ten plagues on to the land of Egypt, until Pharaoh at last agreed to let the people go.

Child   That makes sense, but why do we call this meal Passover?

Leader   Because before the last of the plagues – the death of the Egyptian first-born – God commanded the Israelites to daub the blood of a lamb over their doorposts, as a sign that the plague should pass over their homes and leave their children untouched.

Blessing and sharing of first cup of wine

Leader   In a traditional seder, four cups of wine are drunk, the first called the cup of sanctification and blessing.

Child   Sanctification and blessing – why is it called that?

Leader   It speaks of God's grace, rescuing his people from all that held them captive. It speaks to *us* of redemption from everything that enslaves us in turn, all that destroys and denies life, estranging us from God, obscuring his purpose and frustrating his love. As we drink, we set this occasion apart as something special, consecrated to him in grateful response.

A first cup of wine is poured.

Leader   For the wonder of creation
and your faithfulness across the years,
Lord, we praise you.

All   For your gift of life,
overflowing and abundant,
Lord, we praise you.

All drink.
Traditionally, participants drink while reclining on their left side.

Child   On other nights we eat sitting down, so why tonight do we recline instead?

Leader   Once, when we were slaves, we snatched food whenever we could, eating in haste and discomfort. Now, though, God has given us freedom to enjoy our food and to celebrate at leisure, no longer as slaves or captives, but set at liberty.

The leader takes the shank bone from the ceremonial plate and holds it up for all to see.

Child   What is this bone for? Does it have meaning too?

Leader   It represents the Passover lamb that we spoke of earlier. Through their faithful response to God's command, the people of Israel were passed over by the avenging angel and ultimately delivered from captivity, set free to begin a new life.

The leader takes the egg from the ceremonial plate and again holds it up for all to see.

Child   All right, so what about this egg? Tell me the symbolism of that.

Leader   Having been roasted in fire, it represents all those who have faced the ordeal of grief and mourning, thus offering a reminder of the suffering and sorrow in our world. But eggs also are traditionally a symbol of new life. They speak, then, of the God who offers new life to us and to all.

A song or hymn of praise may be sung at this point.

Blessing and sharing of green vegetable dipped in salty water

The leader holds up a sprig of parsley and a bowl of salty water.

Leader   In our first course we eat green vegetable – parsley – dipped in salty water.

Child   Vegetable in salty water! Why do we eat that?

Leader   The green of parsley reminds us of springtime, symbol of a fresh start, new life bursting out of the ground. It speaks of the renewing power of God, the transformation he brought to the people of

Israel as he led them out of Egypt, and the change he can make in our lives too.

The salty water recalls the tears shed by the people of Israel as they suffered in Egypt – tears of pain, sorrow and despair. It reminds us that as well as springtime there is winter, a truth echoed in our lives, yet even there, it tells us, God is present, at work to bring new life for all.

Leader   Let us thank God for this parsley and water.

All   For your renewing love, Lord,
in good times and bad,
gratefully we worship you.

All take some parsley, dip it into the salty water, and eat it.

Breaking of unleavened bread and hiding of the afikoman

Leader   For our next course we have unleavened bread, or *matzot*.

Child   And what does this mean? On other nights we can eat whatever bread we like, so why tonight do we eat unleavened bread?

Leader   It recalls the time when the people of Israel, waiting in Egypt for their deliverance, were instructed to eat their meal with unleavened bread since there would be no time for them to let bread rise should it be made with leaven. As the Scripture puts it: 'They used the dough they had brought from Egypt to bake unleavened bread; unleavened because there had been insufficient time to add yeast when they fled from Egypt, or to prepare any other provisions.' It is a reminder, then, of God's deliverance, but also of the suffering the Israelites endured before it, the bread therefore being called 'the bread of the affliction'.

It speaks further of God's provision, for leavened bread would quickly have grown stale and mouldy, whereas unleavened bread keeps longer and could, therefore, serve as provisions following the people's flight from Egypt.

And, as we have heard, it represents also lives freed from whatever corrupts and contaminates, separating us from God.

The leader uncovers the unleavened bread, holds up the middle piece, and breaks it into two pieces, setting aside the largest piece to serve as the afikoman and placing the smaller piece between the remaining pieces of bread. The leader then lifts up the tray bearing the bread.

Leader Watch and learn.
Here is the bread of suffering eaten by our forebears in Egypt.
If you are hungry, seeking meaning and purpose in your life, if
you are crushed by heavy burdens, seeking release from your load,
come now and eat, asking that God may redeem you in turn.

All Lord, feed us.

*The leader breaks the bread and distributes it. When everyone is served,
all eat. The leader then lifts up the afikoman and wraps it in a napkin.*

Child Why do you put some bread aside, wrapping it in a napkin?

Leader It is known as the afikoman, and symbolises the fact that the final
fulfilment of God's redemptive purpose is yet to come. Following Passover tradition, we will hide it during the meal.

*The leader passes the afikoman to a helper, whose job it is to hide it
somewhere in the room at an opportune moment. In some seders the
afikoman is broken into several pieces, so that more children can search
successfully. If you follow this practice, you will need a corresponding
number of helpers and 'rewards' rather than just the one.*

Drinking of the second cup of wine

*The leader pours out a second cup of wine, participants, if appropriate,
doing the same.*

Child Why have you poured out more wine? What is the meaning of
this second cup?

Leader It is the cup of deliverance, symbolising the joy of the people of
Israel when God delivered them from Egypt. Yet alongside joy it
also represents sorrow, many recalling as they drink the ten
plagues of Egypt, the suffering caused by Pharaoh's refusal to
obey God's command.
As we drink, then, let us remember those we know for whom
life has brought pain, sadness or hardship.

All drink, reclining as they do so.

A reflective song or hymn may be sung at this point.

The leader puts down the bread and holds up the bitter herbs.

Leader Another ingredient of our meal tonight is bitter herbs.

Child   Bitter herbs! I don't fancy them! Why do you give us those when on other nights we can eat whatever herbs we like?

Leader   They remind us of the bitterness of life endured for so long by the people of Israel until God set them free.

The leader puts down the bitter herbs and holds up the bowl of sweet paste.

Leader   As well as dipping parsley into salty water, we also dip it into this sweet mixture of fruit, nuts, wine and spices.

Child   I'm confused. On other nights we do not season herbs at all, so why tonight do we season them twice?

Leader   Like the salty water this paste speaks of sorrow and hardship, for it represents the clay and straw that the Israelites used in Egypt to make bricks and mortar.

All dip the parsley into the sweet paste, immediately shaking off any residue so that its sweetness cannot hide the bitterness of the herbs.

Leader   May the taste of these herbs help us to empathise
with those whose lot is still bitter to endure,
and to reach out in love towards them.

All   Speak to our hearts,
and inspire us freely and wholeheartedly to respond.

All eat the bitter herbs.

Leader   The hint of sweetness, though, reminds us that God is able to turn those tears to laughter, our sorrow to joy. In other words, our meal speaks of the contrasting sides of life – joy and sorrow, hope and despair, wholeness and suffering, life and death.

The leader takes the remaining portion of unleavened bread and breaks it in two, putting a little bitter herb on one half and placing this back on the ceremonial plate. The leader then holds up the bowl of sweet paste.

Leader   Give thanks for the sweetness of this mixture,
a reminder of hope vindicated,
faith justified as God came to the rescue of his people.

All   Glory to you, sovereign God,
for all this signifies.

All break their piece of bread in two, dip herbs into the sweet paste, place these on top of one piece of the bread, and then place the other piece of bread on top again to make a sandwich.

Leader For the knowledge that you are with us, Lord,
whatever life may bring,
able to turn even the deepest darkness to light,
we praise you.

All In joy or sorrow,
good times or bad,
we will trust you.
Amen.

At this point other food may be shared as a communal meal, boiled eggs often being eaten as the first course. If a full meal is not to be eaten, then a song or hymn of praise could be sung at this point.

The seder meal continues . . .

Drinking of the third cup of wine

The leader pours out the third cup of wine.

Leader We fill now a third cup, the cup of redemption.

Child A third cup? Why do you drink wine again?

Leader Through this cup we thank God for delivering his people, both from captivity and from the angel of death that struck the first-born in Egypt. For us as Christians it takes on extra meaning, calling to mind the sacrifice of Christ, the blood of the new covenant poured out to set us free and bring us life.

All Lord, we thank you.

Leader Let us thank God for this wine.

All Glory to you, God of grace, for your loving provision.

Leader Let us thank God for the new wine of Christ.

All Glory to you, God of grace, for offering life in all its fullness.

All drink the third cup of wine.

The Hallel Psalm

Leader   Let us, then, offer God our worship.

All   Praise the Lord,
give praise to his name.

Leader   Trust in the Lord, people of Israel,
for he is our help and our shield.

All   Praise the Lord,
give praise to his name.

Leader   God has been attentive to our needs,
and will continue to bless us.

All   Praise the Lord,
give praise to his name.

Leader   He grants his blessing to all who fear him,
whatever their status.

All   Praise the Lord,
give praise to his name.

Leader   What can we give back to him
in return for the treasures he has showered upon us?

All   We will lift the cup of salvation,
and call on the name of the Lord.
We will consecrate our lives to worshipping and serving him,
publicly, in the presence of his people, committing ourselves
to his cause.

Leader   We will gladly serve him,
for he has set us free from the cords that bound us.

All   In gratitude we bring him our sacrificial offering,
calling upon his faithful name.

Leader   God is our refuge and our strength.

All   Praise the Lord!
Praise the name of the Lord!
(Adapted from Psalm 113:1; 115:9, 11-13; 116:2, 12, 13, 16a, 17, 19b)

A song or hymn of praise may be sung at this point.

Child   *(pointing to the place laid at the main table but not occupied)*
Why is there a place laid for someone at the table, yet no one sitting there?

Leader   This place is laid for the prophet Elijah.

Child   Elijah? Who's he?

Leader   He was one of the great Old Testament prophets, speaking God's word despite great personal danger, trusting in God despite the way things seemed.

Child   But why set a place for him?

Leader   In Jewish tradition the name of Elijah was associated with the promised Messiah, many expecting that he would be the one to usher in his coming. Leaving room for him symbolises faith in God's continuing purpose.

Child   Is that the only reason?

Leader   No. The place setting reminds us also of our responsibilities towards others: God's call always to be ready to offer hospitality, to give a welcome to the stranger who calls at our door, remembering that we were once strangers in a foreign land.

The fourth cup of wine

The leader pours out a fourth cup of wine.

Child   Another cup of wine? What does this one mean?

Leader   The fourth cup of wine drunk at a traditional seder symbolises thanksgiving and hope. It is a reminder of all God has done, and of all he will yet do.

All   Glory to you, Lord.
Glory and praise to you.
Amen.

All drink.

Child Wait a minute, isn't something missing? What happened to the piece of bread hidden earlier?

Leader Well remembered. We hid that piece as a symbol of hope – a promise that, as God has acted, so he will continue to act, both now and in times to come. The afikoman is indeed hidden, so let any who wish to search, look now. Whoever finds it first will receive a small reward.

Children search for the afikoman, and the one who finds it takes it to the leader, who gives a token reward now or promises to give one after-wards.

Eating of the afikoman

Child Tell me why the bread was hidden.

Leader Some say it is a reminder that God has more yet to do and reveal, but it is also a reminder that worship is a family occasion and should involve fun as well as more serious moments.
  For us, as Christians, it has a special meaning, for it speaks above all of Christ. As bread was broken, so Jesus was broken on a cross. As bread was hidden from view, so his body was laid in a tomb and a stone rolled across the entrance. As bread has been found, so his followers discovered the truth that Jesus was with them once more as the risen Lord.

All After tears came laughter;
after darkness, light;
after doubt, faith;
after despair, hope;
after ends, new beginnings;
after death, life.

Leader Glory to God in the highest.

All Amen.

The afikoman is divided among the participants, this again being eaten while reclining.

A song or hymn of praise may be sung at this point.

The Lord's Supper

Leader A traditional Jewish Passover meal would now be drawing to its close, but as Christians we see Passover in a new light, taking on fuller and deeper meaning in Jesus Christ. We do so because Jesus himself clearly did the same, choosing the time of this festival to also be the time that he would suffer and die.

As the Scriptures tell us: 'On the first day of the Feast of Unleavened Bread Jesus' disciples came to him and asked, "Where would you like us to get things ready so that we can eat the Passover together?" (Matthew 26:17). When the appointed hour came, he and his disciples sat down at the table. Then he told them, "I have yearned to share this Passover meal with you before facing the suffering I must go through, for I will not eat it again until it finds its fulfilment in the kingdom of God."'

All Lord, we also would share Passover with you.

Helpers bring bread and wine to the table. Wafers can, of course, be used if preferred, but the symbolism of a loaf of bread at this point is much more powerful.

The leader breaks the bread into four pieces and places these on to the serving plate.

Child What is the meaning of this bread? Is it the same as the bread we shared earlier?

Leader No, this bread carries for us a different meaning, calling to mind the words and promises of Jesus. 'I am the bread of life,' he told his followers. 'No one who comes to me will ever hunger, and whoever trusts in me will never thirst.'

And then, as he shared Passover with his disciples, he took bread and broke it, saying to them, 'This is my body, broken not for the few but for many.'

All Lord, sustain us through bread of life,
nourishing our souls and bringing fullness of life.

The leader hands the bread to servers to distribute among the participants. Participants stay seated, breaking off a morsel and retaining it until all are served.

Leader Lord Jesus Christ,
knowing what was to come –

your body battered,
broken,
buried –
still you gave thanks to God.

All   We too give thanks.
Amen.

Leader   Eat this,
remembering that Christ died for you.

All   Lord Jesus,
for all you have done, we thank you.

Leader   Eat this,
remembering that through his Spirit he is with us now.

All   Lord Jesus,
for all you continue to do, we praise you.

Leader   Eat this,
remembering his promise to come again.

All   Lord Jesus,
for all you will yet do, we acclaim you.

All eat the bread.

The leader pours wine into a chalice and lifts it up for everyone to see (fill a second chalice or more if necessary).

Child   Why do you pour out wine once more?

Leader   Once more it recalls the words and deeds of Jesus at that last supper with his disciples. 'He took a cup,' we read, 'and, having given thanks, he said, "Take this, and share it among you, for I will not taste the fruit of the vine again until the kingdom has dawned."' It represents his blood, poured out for us and for all.

All   Lord, may the new wine you offer sparkle within us,
coursing through our veins and flowing out to others.

The leader hands the chalice(s) to a helper(s) to serve participants.

Leader Lord Jesus Christ,
knowing the cup you would drink from –
the cup of betrayal and denial,
suffering and death –
still you gave thanks to God.

All We too give thanks.
Amen.

Leader Drink this,
recalling God's gracious dealings in the years gone by.

All Lord Jesus,
we remember.

Leader Drink this,
keeping faith in the present.

All Lord Jesus,
we trust.

Leader Drink this,
anticipating God's future.

All Lord Jesus,
we hope.

All drink.

A song or hymn of praise may be sung at this point.

Leader Through bread and wine we have remembered Christ's love,
his sacrifice,
his pouring himself out for you and for many.

All So, then, we will go out in faith,
with joy and thanksgiving in our hearts,
celebrating what he has done and continues to do,
his love that sets us free,
his purpose that will not be defeated.

Leader The feast is ended.
Go in peace.

All Amen.

A Christian seder meal (3)
The four attitudes

This seder is an abbreviated Christianised adaptation of the Passover Haggadah, making use of the second of the four devices used in a traditional seder to retell the Passover story: the four attitudes. This time it is the congregation who pose questions to the leader, asking how they should respond to four hypothetical cases, and once again we extend this idea as we move into the Lord's Supper.

Welcome and introduction

Leader Why are we here? What are we doing? What is this meal about? You may have come today with all kinds of contrasting feelings: a mixture perhaps of curiosity – wanting to learn and understand more – and scepticism – unsure what point there is in recalling an ancient meal and Festival stemming from a different faith tradition to our own, albeit one to which Christianity owes its existence and in which much of its meaning is found. To a large extent, our attitude will depend upon whether we've shared in an occasion such as this before, and also on how much we know and have understood of the great riches of the Passover story. The more we know of something, the more it makes sense and the more at ease with it we tend to feel. We are also better equipped to make up our mind concerning its relevance to our lives, whether we accept or reject, like or loathe, believe or question it.

Today we are going to explore the meaning of both the Passover meal and the Lord's Supper, exploring some of those mixed feelings and attitudes we've been talking about. A traditional seder celebration skilfully uses these as a way of telling the Passover story, or rather of emphasising its importance. The lessons that come out of all this are equally relevant when it comes to the Lord's Supper or Christian faith itself. Whether the gospel evokes acceptance, hostility, confusion or simply more questions, it is vital when trying to get the message through to focus on the fundamentals. We will never win someone to faith by argument, however clever or persuasive we might be. It is God, and the message of what he has done, that changes lives.

This evening, then, through the elements of the seder and of the Lord's Supper, we reflect on God's dealings with Israel in centuries past, and with all humankind through Jesus Christ.

Lighting of Passover candles

Leader In common with faith traditions across the world, Passover makes room for the symbol of light, it being the custom for a mother or grandmother, as a representative of motherhood, to light candles as symbols of God's love shining into our world and illuminating our hearts. (*Name*) lights the candles for us this evening.

The candles are lit by a mother or grandmother, selected and primed before the service.

Mother Great God,
you have set us apart by your grace,
and we praise you.
We lacked any sense of real identity or purpose,
but you have called us to be your people,
your children,
chosen and precious to you,
and you delight in our presence,
longing for us to know and love you better.
In your name, therefore, we gratefully light these candles,
acknowledging you as the source and spring of life.

All Shine upon us, Lord,
sanctifying our homes, our lives and our world by your presence,
and granting us your blessing and peace,
now and always.

Blessing and sharing of first cup of wine

Leader The first cup in a traditional seder is termed the cup of sanctification and blessing. It is a reminder of God setting Israel apart to be his people, redeemed by his grace and enriched by his goodness. As we drink, we set this occasion apart as something special, consecrated to God in grateful response.

A first cup of wine is poured.

Leader   Let us thank God for this cup and everything it represents.

All   Amen.

Leader   For the events this celebration recalls,
your faithfulness of old,
your delivering your people from oppression in Egypt –

All   Gratefully, Lord, we honour and adore you.

Leader   For your constant love and saving power –

All   Gratefully, Lord, we honour and adore you.

Leader   For the opportunity to share fellowship
with you and one another in this meal –

All   Gratefully, Lord, we honour and adore you.

The cup is passed round and all drink. Traditionally, participants drink while reclining on their left side to symbolise their God-given freedom.

Blessing and sharing of green vegetable dipped in salty water

Leader   Our meal begins with the eating of green vegetable – traditionally parsley. Like all the elements of a seder meal, it is symbolic, the colour green being associated with springtime, and thus speaking of new beginnings. To the eye of faith it points to the renewing and life-giving power of God.

The leader holds up a sprig of parsley.

Leader   Let us ask God's blessing on this parsley,
recognising afresh everything it speaks of.

All   Amen.
Lord, hear us.

Leader   For bringing life out of the earth,
and for bringing us new life –

All   Gracious Lord, we thank you.

Leader We do not eat the vegetable by itself, however, but dip it first in salty water, symbolic this time of the tears shed by the people of Israel as they suffered in Egypt – tears of pain, sorrow and despair.

The leader holds up a bowl of salty water.

Leader Let us ask God's blessing on this salty water,
and everything it represents in turn.

All Amen.
Lord, hear us.

Leader For the knowledge that in joy or sorrow,
pleasure or pain,
you are by our side,
supporting and sustaining,
and looking to see us through –

All Gracious Lord, we thank you.

All take some parsley, dip it into the salty water, and eat it.

Breaking of unleavened bread

Leader We share next in unleavened bread or matzot, the classic symbol of Passover, reminding us of how the Israelites left Egypt in haste and also of the need to purge our lives of all that corrupts and destroys.

The leader uncovers the pieces of bread, holds up the middle piece and breaks it into two pieces, placing these back on to the tray.

Leader Mind this well,
for it represents the bread of affliction eaten by our forebears in Egypt.
Bring your emptiness,
your enslavement to self,
and find freedom,
for God waits to redeem you in turn.

All In faith, Lord, we come.

The leader now sets the tray to one side and pours out a second cup of wine, participants, if appropriate, doing the same. This, however, is not yet drunk.

Telling the story

Leader   Central to any seder meal is the telling and retelling of the Passover story. In a Jewish Passover this is done four times, but this evening we tell the story just once, using the hypothetical cases of four children and the four attitudes they personify.

All   How, then, should we respond to a wise child who asks what God's laws and commandments mean, and why we should keep them?

Leader   You shall teach such a child enthusiastically concerning the events of the Passover and all that God did there for his people – how he saved Moses when Pharaoh ordered the slaughter of new-born Hebrew boys; how, by his providence, Moses was raised in Pharaoh's household, and therefore in a position to return to Egypt in adulthood and seek an audience with Pharaoh; how he demonstrated his sovereign power, humbling Pharaoh and the Egyptians until at last they begged the Israelites to leave.

Tell them all this and more about the way God delivered his people from captivity, sending them out into the wilderness and on to the Promised Land.

All   And how should we respond to the disinterested child, the one who ignores or even mocks this meal, dismissively asking why we eat it?

Leader   You must emphasise all the more what God has done, and strive to bring home to the child that had the Israelites shown such an attitude, God would not have delivered them but would have left them subject to slavery. Remind them that *Pharaoh* would not listen to God's word, and that his people suffered the consequences.

All   What about a child unable to understand – the sort of child who struggles to grasp what the meal or the story is all about?

Leader   With such a child you must keep things simple, not getting bogged down in details but highlighting the key details of what God achieved – how he saw his people's distress and heard their prayer, rescuing them from slavery and sending them out to begin a new life.

All And how, finally, should we respond to the child who, due to a lack of knowledge on the subject, feels unable even to ask a question?

Leader In this case you must patiently, sensitively and lovingly do your best to teach the story of God's faithfulness, doing all you can, through word and deed, to bring the child to understanding. Repeat the story of his love and compassion, his mighty power and his redeeming grace.

Drinking of the second cup of wine

The leader picks up the second cup of wine and holds it up for all to see.

Leader This second cup – the cup of deliverance – is a symbol of joy, recalling God's deliverance of his people. But it is a symbol also of sorrow, for it reminds us of the suffering and evil brought into the world by human sinfulness, these still so much a part of our world today. While there is still heartache and heartbreak around us, our joy cannot be complete.

All Gracious God,
reach out into our broken world,
racked by injustice and exploitation,
suffering and sorrow,
hatred and division.
Reach out,
and bring hope, strength, peace and joy,
by your sovereign grace.
Amen.

Leader Ours is a God who transforms imprisonment to liberty,
tears to laughter,
despair to celebration,
and darkness to light.

All Glory to you, Lord God, ruler over heaven and earth,
for though once we were slaves, now we are free.

All drink the second cup of wine, reclining as they do so.

The leader then picks up the unleavened bread from the ceremonial plate.

Leader   For providing bread out of the dust of the earth . . .

All   Sovereign God, receive our praise.

The leader breaks the top and middle pieces of bread into pieces, and distributes these. Participants retain the bread in their hands until all are served.

Leader   For meeting our innermost needs,
now and for all eternity . . .

All   Sovereign God, receive our praise.

All eat.

Eating of the bitter herbs

Leader   The Scripture instructs us to eat bitter herbs alongside bread. May their taste remind us of all whose lot is bitter still, and of God's call to reach out to them in love.

All dip the bitter herbs into the sweet paste, immediately shaking off any residue so that its sweetness cannot hide the bitterness of the herbs.

All   Whenever life is hard,
wherever there is pain,
be present, O Lord.

All eat the bitter herbs.

Eating of bitter herbs sandwiched in unleavened bread

The leader takes the remaining portion of unleavened bread and breaks it in two, putting a little bitter herb on one half and placing this back on the ceremonial plate. The leader then holds up the bowl of sweet paste.

Leader   This mixture represents the clay and straw used in Egypt to make bricks and mortar, but it reminds us also of the sweetness of hope in God, hope realised as he set them free from slavery.

All   Wherever life is bitter,
its realities harsh,
sweeten it, Lord, through your love.

All take some bread, break it in two, dip herbs into the sweet paste, place these on top of one piece of the bread, and then place the other piece of bread on top again to make a sandwich.

Leader As the Scripture instructs us, we eat the Passover with unleavened bread and bitter herbs.

All Sovereign God,
receive our praise for the deliverance of which this speaks.

All eat, while reclining.

At this point other food may be shared as a communal meal, boiled eggs often being eaten as the first course. The service continues with . . .

Drinking of the third cup of wine

Leader The third cup filled at Passover, the cup of redemption, celebrates God's deliverance of his people, both from the angel of death and from captivity in Egypt.

The leader pours out the third cup of wine.

Leader Hear the word of the Lord.

Reader You have been redeemed from misguided ways of the past, not with silver or gold, the value of which fades, but through the priceless blood of Christ – an unsullied, unblemished lamb.

(1 Peter 1:18, 19)

Leader For this reminder of your deliverance from Egypt . . .

All Gracious Lord, we worship you.

Leader For this reminder of your deliverance in Christ . . .

All Gracious Lord, we worship you.

Leader For this opportunity to remember and to celebrate . . .

All Gracious Lord, we worship you.

Leader For the cup of our salvation . . . .

All Gracious Lord, we worship you.

All drink the third cup of wine.

All Come *to* us, O Lord,
grow *within* us
work *through* us,
and shine *from* us,
through Jesus Christ our Lord.
Amen.

The Hallel Psalm

Leader Let us, then, offer God our worship.

All Amen. Lord, hear us.

Leader Lord, we love you,
for you have listened to our call and responded to our entreaties.

All With heart and soul, we praise you.

Leader Remembering how you gave ear to us,
we will confidently appeal to you again,
trusting you our whole lives long.

All With heart and soul, we praise you.

Leader We despaired of the future,
for the stranglehold of death threatened to overwhelm us,
the prospect of an eternity separated from you looming menacingly,
but when we cried out,
begging you to save us,
you responded to our need.

All With heart and soul, we praise you.

Leader You have granted us light, Lord,
and so we will keep the festival,
and bow down at the altar before you.

All With heart and soul, we worship you.

Leader Praise the Lord!

All   Amen. Praise the Lord!
(Adapted from Psalm 116:1-4; 118:27; 117:2b)

A song or hymn of praise may be sung at this point.

The Lord's Supper

Helpers bring bread and wine to the table. Wafers can, of course, be used if preferred, but the symbolism of a loaf of bread at this point is much more powerful.

Leader   Before breaking bread at Passover it was customary to wash one's hands, thus ensuring ritual purity. Before he broke bread, Jesus went one step further, washing not hands but feet, and not his own but those of Peter, the man he knew would three times deny him. In this demonstration of humility we see the one who comes to serve, to offer his life, to put others before himself; the one who makes *us* clean too, not on the outside but deep within – remade, renewed!

As Jesus tells us: 'The most exalted among you will offer to serve you. Those who sing their own praises will be brought low, but those who show true humility will be lifted high.'
(Matthew 23:11, 12)

At this point the leader may symbolically wash a volunteer's feet (leaders at tables may do likewise).

All   How, then, should we respond to a wise child, one who asks what God's laws and commandments mean, and why we should keep them?

Leader   You shall teach such a child enthusiastically concerning the Lord's life and ministry, and all that God has done for us through him.

All   And how should we respond to the disinterested child, the one who ignores or even mocks this supper, dismissively asking why we eat it?

Leader   You must emphasise all the more what God has done, and strive to bring home to the child that whoever shows such an attitude brings judgement upon themselves, rejecting the new life Christ brings.

All   What about a child unable to understand – the sort of child who struggles to grasp the gospel message?

Leader   With such a child you must keep things simple, not getting side-tracked by incidentals but highlighting the truth that in Christ God has set us free.

All   And how, finally, should we respond to the child who, due to a lack of knowledge on the subject, feels unable even to ask a question?

Leader   In this case, patiently, sensitively and lovingly, you must do your best to lead the child to a saving knowledge of Christ, doing all you can, through word and deed, to kindle faith and understanding.

All   Tell us again, then, the Good News.
Remind us once more of the story.

Reader 1   In the beginning the Word was with God,
and the Word was God.
The Word was made flesh and dwelt among us,
full of grace and truth.

Reader 2   He was born in a stable and laid in a manger,
God's Son, frail and defenceless as a child.

Reader 3   He came to bring light to the world,
but most preferred to walk in darkness.

Reader 1   He came bringing good news to the poor,
release to the captives,
sight to the blind
and freedom to the oppressed –
to proclaim the dawn of God's kingdom.

Reader 2   He was tempted as we are, yet did not fall,
choosing the way of service and sacrifice to redeem the world.

Reader 3   He revealed the extent of God's love,
offering life to all who believe in him.

Reader 1   Betrayed, denied, abandoned, rejected,
he walked the way of the cross to the end,
enduring the agony of death on the cross,
the weight of human sin on his shoulders,
the awfulness of isolation from God his Father.

Reader 2   But he rose again,
triumphant over death,
his love victorious over evil and hatred.

Reader 3   Therefore God exalted him to the heights,
giving him a name above all others,
so that everyone in heaven and on earth
might bend the knee in worship,
each tongue acknowledging him as King of kings
and Lord of lords,
to God's eternal glory.

The leader lifts up the bread for all to see.

Leader   Our Lord Jesus,
on the night of his betrayal,
took bread,
which, after thanking God for it,
he broke, saying,
'This is my body,
broken for you;
do this in memory of me.'

All   Lord, we praise you.

Leader   For bread to feed our body
and living bread to nourish our souls . . .

All   Lord, we praise you.

The leader puts down the bread and pours wine into a chalice (filling a second chalice or more if necessary). The leader then holds up the chalice for all to see.

Leader   In a traditional seder, four cups of wine are drunk, the last being the cup of thanksgiving and joy. Our fourth cup, this evening, is equally a cup of thanksgiving and joy, but it is one imbued by Christ with special meaning, for it speaks not simply of God delivering the Israelites from Egypt but also of him delivering all people from evil, sin and death. As the Scripture puts it: 'He took a cup after supper, saying, "This cup is the new covenant in my blood; whenever you drink it, do so in memory of me."'

Whenever we eat this bread, then, and drink from this cup, we testify to the Lord's death, until he comes.

All   Lord, we thank you.

Leader For the fruit of the vine through which we celebrate,
and for the true vine in which we live and move and have our
being . . .

All Lord, we praise you.

*The leader puts down the chalice and picks up the loaf of bread, breaking
it into four pieces.*

Leader 'My body,' said Jesus,
'broken for you.'

All Lord, we praise you.

*The leader places the chunks of bread on to serving plates, and hands
these to servers to distribute among the participants. Participants stay
seated, breaking off a morsel of bread and retaining it until all are
served.*

Leader Do this in remembrance of me.

All Amen.

All eat the bread. The leader lifts up the chalice for all to see.

Leader 'My blood,' said Jesus,
'poured out for you.'

All Lord, we praise you.

The leader hands the chalice(s) to a helper(s) to serve participants.

Leader 'Do this,' said Jesus,
'in remembrance of me.'

All Amen.

All drink.

Leader In the one who was broken, may we find wholeness.

All In the one whose blood was spilled,
may we find mercy.

Leader   In the one who endured sorrow,
may we find comfort.

All   In the one who faced darkness,
may we find light.

Leader   In the one who suffered hatred,
may we find love.

All   In the one who gave his all,
may we find life in all its fullness.

Leader   The seder was over,
bread shared,
wine poured out,
and then, knowing what the future would hold,
Jesus went out to face the bitterness of Gethsemane,
the agony of the cross.

All   Lord Jesus Christ,
even when life is dark and all seems hopeless,
go with us,
and assure us that even there your purpose continues
and your love will triumph.

Leader   Bread of life,
meet our needs.

All   Broken Christ,
heal our wounds.

Leader   Suffering Saviour,
grant us mercy.

All   Living Lord,
give us life.

Leader   Let us go in peace,
to love and serve the Lord.

All   Amen.

A Christian seder meal (4)
Dayeinu

The following represents another Christianised adaptation of the Passover Haggadah, this time picking up another key strand from within that tradition, the Hebrew response *Dayeinu*, meaning 'It would have been enough' or 'That alone would have been sufficient'. Referring originally to everything God did for the people of Israel in leading them out of Egypt, we develop the response in terms of the gospel, celebrating as we move from the seder into the Lord's Supper everything that God has done for us in Christ.

Welcome and introduction

Leader   What do we mean by a 'Christian seder'? Seder is a Jewish word meaning 'order', and it refers to the general pattern followed during a Passover meal, this having being used for centuries by Jews across the world. Not that there is a set wording for the meal; on the contrary, innovation and creativity have always been encouraged. The general order stays the same, unchanging elements providing the key ingredients to the proceedings, but the way in which this is expressed varies enormously.

Today, though, we are not going to follow the format of a complete Passover meal from start to finish. Why? Partly because as Christians we find new meaning in the Passover outside of Jewish tradition. Partly also because a complete Passover meal coupled with the Lord's Supper would take too long – a seder in itself (even without a full Passover meal) takes several hours. The main reason, however, is that there is so much of spiritual value within a traditional seder that it is worth focusing separately upon each individual aspect, building upon each one in the context of our Christian beliefs and applying them, in particular, to the Lord's Supper. Tonight then, we focus on the so-called *Dayeinu* response – a Hebrew word meaning 'It would have been enough'.

Lighting of Passover candles

Leader   Passover, in common with great religious festivals from many other traditions, makes use of candles to symbolise God's love shining into our world and illuminating our hearts. (*Name*), as a representative of motherhood, lights the candles for us this evening.

The candles are lit by a mother or grandmother, selected and primed before the service.

Mother   Mighty and marvellous God,
sovereign over all,
by your grace you have consecrated us to your service.
Having once been no people,
we are now yours,
called to know and love you,
to bear your name and receive your blessing.
In gratitude we light these candles,
acclaiming you as the source of life,
the beginning and the end,
the giver of all that is, and has been and shall be.

All   Shine in our hearts,
in our homes,
and in our world.
Shine upon us,
within us
and through us,
and, in your mercy, grant us your blessing and peace,
now and always.
Amen.

Blessing and sharing of first cup of wine

Leader   We come now to the first of four cups of wine poured during a conventional seder – the cup of sanctification and blessing. In Jewish tradition, it served as a further reminder of God's calling Israel to be his people and of his blessing them as a nation, supremely, of course, in delivering them from Egypt.

A first cup of wine is poured.

Leader   We see your hand, Lord, in the splendour of the universe
and in the events of history.

All   For your life-giving purpose and redemptive power,
mighty God, we praise you.

Leader   From earliest day you have been at work,
guiding our ancestors,
and delivering our forebears from oppression and captivity.

All   For your life-giving purpose and redemptive power,
mighty God, we praise you.

Leader   You have given us the fruit of the vine,
as a symbol of your creative love
and as a way to celebrate your great goodness.

All   For your life-giving purpose and redemptive power,
mighty God, we praise you.

Leader   As we drink together,
Lord, we consecrate this occasion to you,
setting apart this time and space
in grateful response for all that you have done.

All   For your life-giving purpose and redemptive power,
mighty God, we praise you.

The cup is passed round and all drink. Traditionally, participants drink while reclining on their left side to symbolise their God-given freedom.

Blessing and sharing of green vegetable dipped in salty water

Leader   Our next course, *karpas* – that is, parsley dipped into salty water
– is again redolent with symbolism.

The leader holds up a sprig of parsley.

Leader   The greenness of the parsley calls to mind springtime, and the new birth associated with that season.

The leader holds up a bowl of salty water.

Leader   The salty water recalls the tears shed by the people of Israel as they suffered in Egypt – tears of pain, sorrow and despair.
Let us give thanks for the parsley and the water.

All   For this symbol, Lord, of your creation and re-creation,
of rebirth and new beginnings,
joyfully we worship you.

Leader For this reminder that even in times of pain, sorrow and despair,
you are there,
joyfully we worship you.

All Glory to you, Lord,
for your great faithfulness and constant love.

All take some parsley, dip it into the salty water, and eat it.

Breaking of unleavened bread

Leader In the next part of our seder we share unleavened bread or *mat-zot*. Also known as 'the bread of the affliction', this symbolises the bread made by the Israelites in readiness for the exodus, their flight being conducted in such haste that there was no time for leaven to rise. Furthermore, leavened bread would quickly have perished, whereas unleavened has a much longer life and was thus able to provide sustenance during the early days in the wilderness.

A deeper meaning was drawn from this, leavened bread taken to represent corrupting influences in our lives.

The leader uncovers the unleavened bread, holds up the middle piece, and breaks it into two pieces.

Leader Mark this well.
Here is the bread of affliction eaten by our forebears in Egypt.
Let all who hunger or crave liberation from spiritual enslavement come now and eat,
asking that God may redeem them in turn.

All Amen, Lord. So be it.

Telling the story

Leader Central to any seder meal is the telling and retelling of the Passover story. In a Jewish Passover this is done four times, but this evening we tell the story just once, using the *Dayeinu* formula, a repeated response that emphasises the greatness of God's deliverance. The word, as we noted earlier, means 'It would have been enough' or 'That alone would have been sufficient'. Building on the story of how God called Moses to go before Pharaoh and demand the release of the people of Israel, and of how God subsequently sent ten plagues upon the Egyptians, the last of these – the death of the Egyptian first-born – finally persuading Pharaoh to let the Israelites go, it serves as a refrain of thanksgiving, praise and worship, emphasising the full wonder of all God has done.

The leader picks up the second cup of wine and holds it up for all to see.

Leader This second cup – the cup of deliverance – is a symbol of joy, recalling God's deliverance of his people.
Let us remind ourselves of that story,
putting ourselves as best we can in the shoes of the Israelites so long ago,
and hearing again all that he did for them.

All Amen.

Leader If God had merely rescued us out of the hands of the Egyptians and not revealed the impotence of their idols . . .

All it would have been enough.

Leader If he had merely exposed their gods as worthless and not sent us out loaded with treasures . . .

All it would have been enough.

Leader If he had merely led us empty-handed into the wilderness and not seen us any further . . .

All it would have been enough.

Leader If he had merely parted the waters of the sea and not let us walk across . . .

All it would have been enough.

Leader If he had merely led us safely through to the other side and not obstructed the Egyptians . . .

All it would have been enough.

Leader If he had merely destroyed those who sought to take our lives and not offered further assistance . . .

All it would have been enough.

Leader If he had merely supplied our needs during the long years
in the desert
and not provided divine sustenance . . .

All it would have been enough.

Leader If he had merely given us bread from heaven
and not given us his law . . .

All it would have been enough.

Leader If he had merely given us his commandments on Mount Sinai
and not taken any more interest in our welfare . . .

All it would have been enough.

Leader Yet God did all this and so much more,
blessing us beyond words.

All For his great goodness, we praise him.

The leader holds up the second cup of wine.

Leader It is our duty and delight this evening to worship God,
for he has turned captivity to freedom,
sorrow to joy,
confusion to confidence,
and death to life.

All Glory to you, Lord,
for once we had nothing,
but now we have all.

Leader As well as being a symbol of joy, however, this cup is also a symbol
of sorrow, for it reminds us of the suffering and evil brought into
the world by human sinfulness, these still so much a part of our
world today. While there is still heartache and heartbreak around
us, our joy cannot be complete.

So, then, let us pray for our world in all its need.

All Lord Jesus Christ,
Light of the world,

reach out in love,
and wherever life is dark
may your grace bring a new dawn.

Leader Lord of all,
Lamb of God,
reach out in love,
and wherever there is hurt and suffering
may your grace bring healing.

All Lord of all,
bread of life,
reach out in love,
and wherever people search for meaning
may your grace nourish them.

Leader Lord of all,
new and living wine,
wherever life has lost its sparkle
may your love rekindle joy.

All Lord of all,
the resurrection and the life,
wherever death casts its shadow
may your love bring the promise of eternal blessing.

Leader Lord, hear us.

All Amen.

All drink the second cup of wine, reclining as they do so. The leader then picks up the unleavened bread from the ceremonial plate.

Leader Glory to you, Lord of all,
for bringing bread from the earth.

The leader breaks the top and middle pieces of bread into pieces, and distributes these. Participants retain the bread in their hands until all are served.

All Glory to you, Lord,
for feeding us in body, mind and spirit.

All eat.

Eating of the bitter herbs

The leader holds up bitter herbs and the bowl of sweet paste.

Leader   As the Scripture instructs us, as well as bread we eat bitter herbs, recalling the bitterness of life endured by the people of Israel in Egypt. We dip the herbs into this mixture, a reminder of the clay and straw used in Egypt to make bricks and mortar.

All dip the bitter herbs into the sweet paste, immediately shaking off any residue so that its sweetness cannot hide the bitterness of the herbs.

Leader   May the taste of these herbs help us to empathise with those whose lot is still bitter to endure, and to respond in God's name.

All   Wherever life is hard, Lord,
teach us to reach out in love.

All eat the bitter herbs.

Eating of bitter herb sandwiched in unleavened bread

The leader takes the remaining portion of unleavened bread and breaks it in two, putting a little bitter herb on one half and placing this back on the ceremonial plate. The leader then holds up again the bowl of sweet paste.

Leader   This mixture has reminded us of sorrow and oppression, but its sweetness reminds us also of joy brought by hope in God; a hope realised for the people of Israel as he set them free from slavery.

All   Glory to you, sovereign God,
for this mixture
and all it signifies.

All take some bread, break it in two, dip herbs into the sweet paste, place these on top of one piece of the bread, and then place the other piece of bread on top again to make a sandwich.

Leader   As it is written: 'They shall eat unleavened bread and bitter herbs.'

All   We eat, Lord, with thanksgiving.

All eat, while reclining.

At this point other food may be shared as a communal meal, boiled eggs often being eaten as the first course. The service continues . . .

Leader   We have remembered and celebrated the events of Passover, but, of course, this is not a Passover celebration as such but an interpretation reflecting our faith in Christ. For us, what God did for the people of Israel in Egypt was, if you like, a foretaste of a greater deliverance yet to come, a deliverance not of the few but *all*, breaking the bonds of evil and human sin and thus setting us free from whatever prevents us enjoying the new life God longs for us to enjoy. As we continue, then, with the meal, we will relate all we do more fully to Christ, celebrating what God has done and all he offers through him.

Drinking of the third cup of wine

Leader   We fill now a third cup – the cup of redemption that, for the people of Israel, served as a reminder of how God delivered them from the shadow of death and the torment of captivity.

The leader pours out the third cup of wine.

Leader   Honour and praise to you, sovereign God,
for delivering your people from Egypt.

All   Glory to you for fruit of the vine.

Leader   Honour and praise to you, sovereign God,
for delivering your people through Christ.

All   Glory to you for new life through him.

Leader   Honour and praise to you, sovereign God,
for allowing us to share in this special feast,
as generations have shared before us.

All   Glory to you for inviting us to share at the Lord's table,
as part of your people in every age and time.

All drink the third cup of wine.

Leader   May the God of love guide our footsteps in the way of peace
this and every day.

All   Amen. So be it.

The Hallel Psalm

Leader   Let us, then, offer God our worship.

All   God is good;
give thanks to him,
for his love is constant,
enduring for eternity.

Leader   In his mighty wisdom, he created the universe,
the sun, moon and stars,
galaxies and constellations,
space in all its vastness.

All   Give thanks to him,
for his love is constant,
enduring for eternity.

Leader   He fashioned the earth,
the sea and the dry land,
all was made by him.

All   Give thanks to him,
for his love is constant,
enduring for eternity.

Leader   He stretched out his arm,
and with a mighty hand rescued Israel from Egypt.

All   Give thanks to him,
for his love is constant,
enduring for eternity.

Leader   He divided the waters of the Red Sea,
enabling the people to walk through it to safety,
afterwards engulfing those who pursued them.

All   Give thanks to him,
for his love is constant,
enduring for eternity.

Leader   He led his people through the desert,
and gave them the land as their inheritance.

All   Give thanks to him,
for his love is constant,
enduring for eternity.

Leader   He reaches out to all who recognise their need,
rescuing,
leading,
providing,
blessing.

All   Give thanks to him,
for his love is constant,
enduring for eternity.

Leader   Great is the Lord,
and wonderful are his deeds.

All   Joyfully, we give him thanks,
for his love is constant,
enduring for eternity.

Leader   Praise the Lord!

All   Amen. Praise the Lord!
(Adapted from Psalm 136 and Psalm 117:2b)

A song or hymn of praise may be sung at this point.

The fourth cup of wine

The leader pours out a fourth cup of wine.

Leader   The fourth cup of wine drunk at a traditional seder symbolises
thanksgiving and hope. It is a reminder of all God has done, and
of all he will yet do.

All   Glory to you, Lord.
Glory and praise to you.
Amen.

All drink.

The Lord's Supper

Leader　If we were following a traditional Passover seder, our meal now would be nearly at an end, but this is a Christian seder and the main course is yet to come.

Through breaking bread and sharing wine at Passover, of all occasions, Jesus purposely imbued it with new meaning, presenting himself as the fulfilment of that ancient festival – the Lamb of God bringing deliverance, freedom, hope and new life for his people. As the Scriptures put it: '"I tell you this," said Jesus, "you do not have life in you unless you eat the flesh of the Son of Man and drink his blood. My flesh is true food, and my blood true drink. Those who eat my flesh and drink my blood possess eternal life and at the end of time I will raise them up. They will live in me, and I in them."'

Helpers bring bread and wine to the table. Wafers can, of course, be used if preferred, but the symbolism of a loaf of bread at this point is much more powerful.

Leader　Lord Jesus, had you loved us only so much as to share our life –
entering our world,
shining in our darkness,
preaching and teaching your word . . .

All　it would have been enough.

Leader　Had you loved us only so much as to share your love –
healing the sick,
comforting the broken,
giving hope to the oppressed . . .

All　it would have been enough.

Leader　Had you loved us only so much as to share our death –
dying on a cross,
bearing our sins,
enduring darkness and despair . . .

All　it would have been enough.

Leader　Yet you love us so much that you did more than all that,
sharing *your* life,
life eternal,
abundant,
brimming over in all its fullness,
beyond our finest words or wildest imagining.

All   It is enough,
and more than enough!
Lord, we thank you.
Amen.

Leader   Hear then the words of Scripture, recalling the Passover Jesus shared with his Apostles.

    'During supper, he took bread, and, having given thanks, he broke it and gave it to them, saying, "Take this; it is my body." Then he took a cup, and, giving thanks to God, he handed it to them, and they all drank from it. Then he said, "This is my blood, the blood of the covenant, shed for many. I tell you the truth, I will not drink of the fruit of the vine again until that day when I drink it new with you in the kingdom of God."'

The leader lifts up the bread for all to see.

Leader   For all that bread meant to the people of Israel –
symbol of deliverance,
reminder of Passover . . .

All   Sovereign God, we thank you.

Leader   For all that bread means to *us* –
symbol of Christ's sacrifice,
token of his broken body . . .

All   Sovereign God, we thank you.

The leader puts down the bread and pours wine into a chalice (filling a second chalice or more if necessary). The leader then holds up the chalice for all to see.

Leader   For all that wine has meant across the centuries,
symbol of fruitfulness,
means of celebration . . .

All   Sovereign God, we thank you.

Leader   For all that wine means to *us*,
symbol of Christ's blood shed for all,
sign of new beginnings . . .

All   Sovereign God, we thank you.
Amen.

The leader puts down the chalice and picks up the loaf of bread, breaking it into four pieces.

Leader   Broken bread,
God's gift,
offered to you.

All   Lord, we thank you.

The leader places the chunks of bread on to serving plates, and hands these to servers to distribute among the participants. Participants stay seated, breaking off a morsel of bread and retaining it until all are served.

Leader   His body was broken –
for you,
for me,
for all.

All eat the bread.

The leader lifts up the chalice for all to see.

Leader   Poured out wine,
God's gift,
offered to you.

All   Lord, we thank you.

The leader hands the chalice(s) to a helper(s) to serve participants.

Leader   His blood was shed,
for all,
for me,
for you.

All   Lord, we thank you.

All drink.

Leader   In bread and wine,
recognise the one who endured sorrow to bring us joy,
despair to bring us hope
and death to bring us life.

All   Lord Jesus Christ,
to you be glory and honour,
worship and acclamation.

Leader   God of the Passover,
delivering your people from captivity in Egypt
and leading them through the wilderness into the Promised Land,
go with us now.

All   God of the new Passover,
delivering us from slavery to sin and self,
and leading us throughout our journey of faith
into newness of life,
go with us now and always.
Amen.

Leader   Let us go in peace,
to love and serve the Lord.

All   Amen.

A Christian seder meal (5)
The k'arah symbols

The following is another abbreviated Christian seder, this time picking up the final way in which the story of the Passover is told during a traditional meal; namely, through explaining the significance of the principal symbols placed upon the ceremonial plate, or k'arah, used in the meal.

Welcome and introduction

Leader   Welcome to this celebration of what we have termed 'a Christian seder'. If you're wondering precisely what this means, let me explain. The word seder means order and describes the pattern used for centuries by Jews across the world to celebrate the Passover meal. There is no set form of seder that all are expected to follow. On the contrary, the Passover tradition encourages innovation and creativity, so numerous orders have been devised, adapted for different times, places and situations, just as we adapt ours today to express our faith in Christ as the ultimate fulfilment of God's redemptive purpose.

Out of respect to Jewish believers, it is important to recognise at the outset that what we will be sharing this evening cannot be equated to a Passover meal as it is traditionally understood. While we will use ideas, words and customs derived from this, we will do so in the light of Christ, adapted to reflect our convictions concerning his significance for us and for all. Do not think, though, that this free use of the Passover is a modern invention, for it was begun by Christ himself. A Jew himself, he would have participated in numerous Passover meals during his lifetime, the last of those being the supper he shared with his disciples in the upper room – what we today call Holy Communion, Eucharist, Mass, or simply the Lord's Supper. Through breaking bread and sharing wine at Passover, of all occasions, Jesus purposely imbued it with new meaning, presenting himself as the fulfilment of that ancient festival – the Lamb of God bringing deliverance, freedom, hope and new life to his people. In understanding this symbolism, our faith can only be deepened and enriched.

This evening, then, we will explore the last of the four key teaching devices used in a traditional Passover celebration:

namely, focusing on and explaining the symbols used on the so-called k'arah – the ceremonial plate used in a seder meal. We will then reflect in turn upon the symbols used in a celebration of Holy Communion.

Lighting of Passover candles

Leader In keeping with the Passover tradition, we now light candles, their flame reminding us of God's love shining in Christ, the Light of the World, and light of our lives.

(*Name*), as a representative of motherhood, lights the candles for us this evening.

The candles are lit by a mother or grandmother, selected and primed before the service.

Mother Glory to you, mighty and marvellous God,
for you have set us apart by your grace.
Once we were no people,
but you have called us to know and love you.
In your name we light these candles,
acknowledging you as the giver and sustainer of life.

All Lord, shine upon us.
May your radiance brighten our homes,
enrich our lives
and illumine our world,
your blessing and peace going with us,
now and always.

Blessing and sharing of first cup of wine

A first cup of wine is poured.

Leader In a traditional seder, four cups of wine are drunk, the first of which is called the cup of sanctification and blessing. It speaks of God's grace, rescuing his people from all that held them captive. It speaks to *us* of redemption from everything that enslaves us in turn, all that destroys and denies life, estranging us from God, obscuring his purpose and frustrating his love. As we drink, we set this occasion apart as something special, consecrated to him in grateful response.

All   For this cup, Lord,
and all it symbolises,
receive our praise.

All drink. Traditionally, participants recline on their left side while doing so, thus symbolising their God-given freedom.

Telling the story

Leader   Central to any seder meal is the telling and retelling of the Passover story. In a Jewish Passover this is done four times but this evening, as explained earlier, we use just the last method, enlarging on the Passover story through exploring the meaning of the k'arah symbols – the elements placed on the Passover plate. Tradition tells us that if we fail to explain the meaning of these, then we are failing in our duty and not properly celebrating the feast.

Blessing and sharing of green vegetable dipped in salty water

The leader holds up a sprig of parsley.

Leader   One of the many symbolic foods eaten at Passover is what the Jews call karpas; in other words, green vegetable, traditionally parsley.

All   Tell us why we eat this.

Leader   The greenness of the vegetable calls to mind springtime, and offers a reminder of new birth and new beginnings.
    To us, as Christians, it speaks of the new life God has given us in Christ.

The leader holds up a bowl of salty water.

Leader   Alongside the promise of springtime, however, we have another symbol – salty water. It recalls the tears shed by the people of Israel as they suffered in Egypt – tears of pain, sorrow and despair. We are reminded, then, that alongside joy life brings sadness, alongside spring, winter.

All   In joy or sorrow,
pleasure or pain,

you are there,
striving to fulfil your loving purpose.
Glory to you, O God.

All take some parsley, dip it into salty water, and eat it.

Breaking of unleavened bread and hiding of the afikoman

The leader holds up one of the portions of unleavened bread.

Leader In this next part of our seder we make use of another symbol, unleavened bread.

All Why unleavened rather than leavened bread?

Leader Traditionally called 'bread of the affliction', or *matzot* in Hebrew, it recalls the haste with which the people of Israel finally left Egypt. As the Scripture (Exodus 12:39) puts it: 'They used the dough they had brought from Egypt to bake unleavened bread; unleavened because there had been insufficient time to add yeast when they fled from Egypt, or to prepare any other provisions.'
Three pieces are used in all, two representing those placed in the temple at Jerusalem during the Festival, and the third – placed between the two others – broken in half during the meal.

The leader breaks the bread in half, setting aside the largest piece to serve as the afikoman.

Leader Mark this carefully!
Here is the bread of suffering eaten by our forebears in Egypt.
Are you hungry,
searching for spiritual fulfilment,
craving freedom from all that holds you captive?
Then come now and eat,
for God waits to redeem you in turn.

All Amen, Lord. So be it.

The leader lifts up the afikoman, wraps it in a napkin and passes it to a helper, whose job it is to hide it somewhere in the room at an opportune moment. In some seders it is broken into several pieces, so that more children can search successfully. If you follow this practice, you will need a corresponding number of helpers and 'rewards' rather than just the one.

Leader   It is traditional within a Passover meal to hide part of the broken bread, known as the afikoman, young children present having the opportunity to find this later.

All   What is the meaning of this?

Leader   Some suggest that this practice symbolises the Jews' expectation of the Messiah, though its chief purpose is far more prosaic, being simply to hold the interest of children present and keep them awake! As Christians, however, as we shall see later, we find much deeper symbolism here.

The leader then picks up a second portion of unleavened bread from the ceremonial plate, breaks it up and distributes the pieces among partici-pants. Participants retain the bread in their hands until all are served.

Leader   Glory to you, creator God,
for you bring bread from the earth.

All   Glory to you, Lord,
for providing bread and nourishment.

All eat.

A hymn or song may be sung at this point

The leader pours out a second cup of wine, participants topping up their cups in turn.

Leader   This second cup – the cup of deliverance – is a symbol of joy, recalling God's deliverance of his people. But it is a symbol also of sorrow, for it reminds us of the misery brought into the world by human sinfulness, the suffering, evil and tragedy endured by so many, these still as much a part of our world today as ever.

All   While there is still heartache and heartbreak around us, our joy cannot be complete.

Leader   Nonetheless, we celebrate what God has done – for his people of old and for us today – how he has transformed imprisonment to liberty, tears to laughter, despair to celebration, and darkness to light.

All   Glory to you, redeeming God,
for the freedom you have brought us.

Leader   Remembering what God has done for us,
let us, then, pray for others.

All   Sovereign God,
come now into the darkness of our world:
into the night-time of suffering and sickness,
doubt and despair,
hurt and heartbreak,
injustice and evil,
violence and hatred,
fear and death.
Come now,
and bring your deliverance.
Amen.

All drink the second cup of wine, reclining as they do so.

The leader takes the shank bone from the ceremonial plate and holds it up for all to see.

All   What does this bone symbolise?

Leader   It represents the Passover lamb, a reminder of the lambs sacrificed in Egypt in obedience to God's commands, thus indicating to the avenging angel that it should *pass over* the homes of the Israelites.
 For us as Christians the Passover lamb takes on new significance in Christ, the one whose blood was shed to bring us freedom and new life. We see in him the definitive sacrifice, offered so that we might also become his people, chosen and precious to him.

All   For your grace, Lord, we thank you.

The leader takes the roasted egg from the ceremonial plate and again holds it up for all to see.

All   An egg? Does this have meaning too?

Leader   This roasted egg, or beitzah, symbolises distress and despair, but also new beginnings. Having been roasted in fire, it represents all those who have faced the ordeal of grief and mourning, thus offering a reminder of the suffering and sorrow in our world. But eggs also are traditionally a symbol of new life. They speak, then, of the God who offers new life to us and to all.

All   For your renewing power, Lord, we thank you.

Eating of bitter herbs sandwiched in unleavened bread

The leader holds up the bitter herbs.

Leader The Scripture instructs us to eat bread with bitter herbs.

All Tell us what the herbs signify.

Leader Known by the Jews as maror, they represent the bitterness of life endured by the people of Israel under Egyptian oppression. As the Scripture (Exodus 1:13, 14) puts it: 'The Egyptians ruthlessly imposed ever more demanding tasks upon the Israelites, forcing them to make bricks and work the fields, their lives made bitter by hard labour.'

The leader then holds up the bowl of sweet paste.

Leader Before we eat the herbs we dip them briefly into a sweet mixture of fruit, nuts, wine and spices.

All Tell us more about this mixture.

Leader The Jews call it charoset. Like the salty water this paste speaks of sorrow and hardship, for it represents the clay and straw that the Israelites used in Egypt to make bricks and mortar.

All dip the bitter herbs into the sweet paste, immediately shaking off any residue so that its sweetness cannot hide the bitterness of the herbs.

Leader May the bitterness of these herbs help us to think of those for whom life is bitter today.

All May it inspire us, Lord, to reach out in love,
in your name.

All eat the bitter herbs.

The leader takes the remaining portion of unleavened bread and breaks it in two, putting a little bitter herb on one half and some more herbs, this time dipped and covered in the sweet paste, on top of this. Finally, the other half of the bread is placed on top again to make a sandwich. Participants do the same.

Leader The sweetness of this paste, however, reminds us that God is able to turn tears to laughter, our sorrow to joy. In other words, this part of our meal speaks of the contrasting sides of life – joy and sorrow, hope and despair, wholeness and suffering, life and death.

All   We eat, Lord, with thanksgiving.

All eat, while reclining.

Drinking of the third cup of wine

The leader pours out the third cup of wine.

Leader   We fill now a third cup, the cup of redemption. It celebrates God's deliverance of his people, both from the plague of death that struck the Egyptian first-born and from their long years of slavery.

For us, as Christians, that deliverance comes definitively in Christ, who gave his all to set us free from whatever denies and destroys life.

All   Amen. Lord, we thank you.

Leader   You are worthy, O Lord our God,
to receive glory and honour and power,
for all things were made by you,
their creation and existence down to your sovereign will.

All   Glory to you, living God,
for this cup celebrating the deliverance of your people.

All drink the third cup of wine.

The Hallel Psalm

Leader   Let us, then, offer God a psalm of praise.

All   Lord, hear us.

Leader   The Lord is full of grace and mercy,
dependable and honourable in all he does.

All   He protects the humble,
and, when life puts us on our knees, he picks us up again.

Leader   Let our souls be at peace and our minds at rest,
for God is generous in all his dealings.

All   He has rescued our souls from death,
wiped tears away from our eyes
and prevented us from stumbling.

Leader   Though times have been hard,
testing belief to the limit,
he has helped us to hold on to our faith.

All   Bemused and bewildered,
we have nonetheless trusted in his love,
despite those who would deny it.

Leader   At times life pushed us right to the edge,
so that we felt we were going under,
yet when we needed him most, he was there,
coming to our assistance.

All   The Lord is our help and strength –
he has brought us salvation.

Leader   With him walking by our side,
we are able to live to the full.

All   You are our God, and we thank you for it.
We will shout your name from the rooftops.

Leader   Praise the Lord!

All   Amen. Praise the Lord!
(Adapted from Psalm 116:5-11; 118:13, 14, 28; 117:2b)

A song or hymn of praise may be sung at this point.

The fourth cup of wine

The leader pours out a fourth cup of wine.

Leader   The fourth cup of wine drunk at a traditional seder symbolises
thanksgiving and hope. It is a reminder of all God has done, and
of all he will yet do.

All   Glory to you, Lord.
Glory and praise to you.
Amen.

All drink.

At this point other food may be shared as a communal meal, boiled eggs often being eaten as the first course. Alternatively, a hymn or song may be sung. The seder then continues . . .

Leader   Though near its close, a traditional Passover meal would at this point be incomplete, for, as you may have noticed, something is missing.

All   Yes, what happened to the piece of bread you broke off and wrapped up earlier?

Leader   Some say it is a reminder that God has more yet to do and reveal, but it is also a reminder that worship is a family occasion and should involve fun as well as more serious moments. So, then, let all who wish to take part search now for the afikoman. A small reward will be given to whoever is first to find it.

Adapt the above wording if you have broken the portion of afikoman into several pieces.

Children search for the afikoman, and the one(s) who finds it takes it to the leader, who gives a reward now or promises one later.

Eating of the afikoman

Leader   For us, as Christians, this afikoman has special meaning, for it speaks above all of Christ. As bread was broken, so Jesus was broken on a cross. As bread was hidden from view, so his body was laid in a tomb and a stone rolled across the entrance. As bread has been found, so his followers discovered the truth that Jesus was with them once more as the risen Lord.

There is more still to discover today, for though in Christ we see and know God, our knowledge is still incomplete; there is always more to learn, more to experience, more to be revealed.

All   Lord Jesus Christ,
we meet you and greet you.
Lead us into a greater awareness of your love,
deeper insight into truth,
and a fuller experience of life.
Amen.

The afikoman is divided among the participants, this again being eaten while reclining.

Another hymn or song may be sung at this point.

The Lord's Supper

Leader As Jesus would have been well aware, having celebrated the Passover many times himself, the meal at this point would have been almost over. But we are sharing today in a Christian seder, instituted personally by Christ and celebrated in simple form week by week in what we know as the Lord's Supper. The time he chose, the elements he shared, the words he used, and the events that ensued, leave us in no doubt that he intended us to understand his life and ministry, and in particular his death, in terms of the Passover, his suffering and sacrifice giving new and yet more redolent meaning to the powerful symbolism of that festival.

Helpers bring bread and wine to the table. For this service, cover both with a white cloth, to be removed during the explanation of what bread and wine symbolise. Rather than use wafers, a loaf of bread should be used at this point, its symbolism being much more powerful.

Leader Before breaking bread at Passover it was customary to wash one's hands, thus ensuring ritual purity. Before he broke bread, Jesus went one step further, washing not hands but feet, and not his own but those of Peter, the man he knew would three times deny him. In this demonstration of humility we see the one who came to serve, to offer his life, to put others before himself; the one who makes *us* clean too, not on the outside but deep within – remade, renewed!

At this point the leader may symbolically wash a volunteer's feet (leaders at tables may do likewise).

Leader The symbols of bread and wine are no doubt familiar to us all, but how often do we pause to consider what they represent? If we fail to explain their meaning, then we are failing in our duty and not properly celebrating the feast.

The bread is uncovered and held up for all to see.

Leader This represents the body of Christ, his flesh lacerated by the whip, pierced by thorns on his head, nails in his hands and feet, and a spear in his side. As the Scriptures tells us (Isaiah 53:5a): 'He was wounded for our transgressions, crushed for our iniquities.'

All   Lord, we thank you.

Leader   It speaks of spiritual sustenance, an answer to our spiritual hunger, true and lasting fulfilment. As Jesus said (John 6:35a): 'I am the bread of life; no one who comes to me will ever hunger.'

All   Lord, we thank you.

Leader   It speaks of unity in Christ, the fact that we eat from the same loaf symbolising the fellowship he wants us to share in him. As the Scriptures put it once more: 'Is not this bread we break together a sharing in the body of Christ? Since we share together in the one loaf, despite being many we are one body.'

All   Lord, we thank you.

The leader uncovers the wine and holds it up for all to see.

Leader   This represents the blood of Christ, spilled from his head, his hands, his feet, his side, poured out like the blood of the Passover lamb. As the Scripture tells us (Hebrews 9:12): 'Christ went irreversibly into the Holy of holies, offering not goats' blood or that of calves, but his own blood, through which he has secured for us everlasting salvation.'

All   Lord, we thank you.

Leader   It speaks of new life, bubbling over, sparkling with promise. As the Scripture says (John 2:10): 'Most people serve the quality wine first, and then make do afterwards, but you have saved the very best until now!'

All   Lord, we thank you.

Leader   It speaks also of being one with Christ, rooted in him, nourished and nurtured by his grace, so that our lives might bear fruit in his service. As the Scripture has it (1 Corinthians 10:16a): 'This cup of blessing for which we give thanks, do we not share through it in the blood of Christ.' And as Jesus put it, speaking to his disciples (John 15:5): 'I am the true vine, you are the branches. If you abide in me and I in you, then your lives will be truly fruitful.'

All   Lord, we thank you.

Leader While they were eating together, Jesus took bread, blessed and broke it, and then handed it to his disciples with the words: 'Take and eat, for this is my body.' Afterwards, he took a cup, gave thanks for it, and passed it to them, saying: 'Drink from this, each one of you, for it is my blood of the new covenant, poured out for you and for many, to make possible forgiveness for all.'

The leader again lifts up the bread for all to see.

Leader For this bread, Lord,
and all it represents . . .

All Receive our praise.

The leader puts down the bread and pours wine into a chalice (filling a second chalice or more if necessary). The leader then holds up the chalice for all to see.

Leader For this wine,
and all it represents . . .

All Receive our praise.

The leader puts down the chalice, picks up the loaf of bread, breaks it into four pieces and places the chunks on to serving plates, handing these to servers to distribute among the participants. Participants stay seated, breaking off a morsel of bread and retaining it until all are served.

Leader Eat this,
remember what Christ has done,
and through receiving him afresh into your life
find nourishment for your soul;
your hunger satisfied.

All Amen. Lord, we thank you.

All eat the bread.

The leader lifts up the chalice for all to see.

Leader The cup of our salvation,
poured out,
brimming over.

All Amen. Lord, we thank you.

The leader hands the chalice(s) to a helper(s) to serve participants.

Leader Drink this,
remember what Christ has done,
and through consecrating your life to his service
find true and lasting fulfilment,
your thirst quenched.

All Amen. Lord, we thank you.

All drink.

Leader 'I tell you this,' said Jesus, 'you do not have life in you unless you eat the flesh of the Son of Man and drink his blood. My flesh is true food, and my blood true drink. Those who eat my flesh and drink my blood possess eternal life and at the end of time I will raise them up. They will live in me, and I in them' (John 6:53-56).

May Jesus Christ,
the source, pattern and giver of life,
sustain and keep you
as you walk in his way
and offer him your service.

All Amen.

Appendix 1
Recipes for elements of a full seder meal

There are innumerable recipes for dishes to include in a full seder meal (see last entry in Appendix 2). Below I give recipes simply for three of the most commonly eaten and traditional dishes, but if you are planning a full meal you will want to do your own research and include others.

Charoset   For use within the symbolic part of the seder meal.

Makes approximately 60 teaspoonfuls.

Ingredients
3 chopped dessert apples
1 small cup walnuts
1 small cup chopped dates and/or figs
4 tbsp wine (or grape juice if you prefer to avoid using alcohol)
2 tsp honey
2 tsp wine vinegar (red if possible)
1 tsp ground cinnamon
$1/4$ cup raisins
$1/4$ cup sultanas
$1/4$ tsp ground cloves
1 tsp lime or lemon juice

Method
Peel and core the apples, then cut up into small chunks. Mix with the dates, figs, raisins and sultanas, and grind very briefly in a food processor. Add the remaining ingredients and stir well. Other fruits can be added, as desired.

Gefilte Fish   To be served as a starter.

Makes 20-25 small balls.

Ingredients
4lbs white fish (carefully filleted, then ground)
3-4 carrots, sliced

1 onion, chopped
1 egg
$^1\!/_2$ cup fish stock
$^1\!/_2$ cup matzot meal
small pat of margarine
2 tbsp sugar
pinch of salt
pinch of pepper

Method

Mix onion with margarine. Mix carrots, egg, meal, sugar, stock and seasoning with the ground fish. Stir in the onion, and then form into small balls. Bring to the boil in water, then simmer for 2 hours. Serve.

Matzot Balls   To be served as an accompaniment to chicken soup, as a starter.

Makes approximately 20-25 balls.

Ingredients
6 large eggs
$1^1\!/_2$ cups matzot meal
1 tsp salt
$^1\!/_4$ tsp pepper
2 tbsp water
$^1\!/_2$ cup melted margarine (optional)

Method

Blend the meal with the salt, pepper and water. Separate the eggs, and beat the whites in the melted margarine, until the mixture thickens. Beat the yolks until they become creamy. Stir the blended matzot into the beaten yolks, then add to the egg-white mixture. Mix well, then set aside in a refrigerator for a good hour. Afterwards, shape the mixture into small balls. Boil these in salted water (or in chicken soup) for at least twenty minutes or until the balls have become soft. Finally, either store the balls in the soup or water, or freeze them, until it is time to serve.

Appendix 2
Useful websites

There are innumerable sites online where information can be found concerning the Passover, many providing seder texts from within the Jewish tradition and other Christian versions of a seder meal. In preparing this book I found the following particularly useful:

- 'Text of the Passover Haggadah' – a full version in English of the Passover Haggadah, published by the Kehot Publication Society.
  See www.sichosinenglish.org/cgi-bin/calendar?holiday= pesach11101

- 'Introduction to a Christian Seder' – comprehensive introduction to the Passover festival, together with an overview of the seder meal and how to stage it, written by Dennis Bratcher.
  See www.cresourcei.org/haggadah.html

- 'Preparing for a Passover Seder' – comprehensive guidelines, as its title suggests, for staging a seder meal, written by David Sargent.
  See www.godandscience.org/apologetics/seder.html

- 'The Passover Seder for Christians' – a fully worked-out adaptation of the seder, written by Dennis Bratcher.
  See www.cresourcei.org/haggadah.html

- 'Passover Seder Companion' – a small but useful site giving elucidating commentary on every stage of the seder.
  See www.chabad.org./holidays/passover/pesach.asp?AID= 1759

- 'The Passover Meal: A Ritual for the Christian Home' – written by Arleen Hynes, this provides comprehensive background information to the Passover coupled with excellent practical suggestions towards staging a Christian seder.
  See www.ewtn.com/library/ FAMILY/PASSMEAL.TXT

- 'Women for Faith and Family' – a Christian Passover seder for Holy Thursday.
  See www.wf-f.org/Seder.html

- 'Everything Passover' – a site answering just about every query you might ever have about Passover, or indeed about all things Jewish.
  See www.machers.com/directory/Holidays_and_Observances/Passover/index.html

- 'Learn about Passover: to ask Moses' – another Jewish site, full of useful information about Passover and Judaism as a whole.
  See www.askmoses.com

- 'Happy Pesach – Happy Passover!' – an extensive website giving answers to just about every conceivable question concerning Passover, together with a list of all sites that provide seder meal recipes.
  See www.angelfire.com/pa2/passover/passoverrecipes.html